THE HANGOVER COMPANION

A Guide to the Morning After

THE HANGOVER COMPANION

A Guide to the Morning After

Michael O'Mara Books Limited

First published in Great Britain in 2006 by
Michael O'Mara Books Limited
9 Lion Yard
Tremadoc Road
London SW4 7NQ

A CIP catalogue record for this book is available from the British Library

ISBN 10: 1-84317-213-5
ISBN 13: 978-1-84317-213-0

10 9 8 7 6 5 4 3 2 1

Designed and typeset by Design 23

Illustrations from www.shutterstock.com

Printed in Great Britain by William Clowes Ltd, Beccles, Suffolk

CONTENTS

*Woe unto them
that rise up
early in the
morning, that
they may follow
strong drink.*

ISAIAH 5:11

Introduction

Hangovers get a mention in the Bible? That just goes to show how we've been suffering from them for as long as anyone can remember – anyone who was sober last night, that is, not anyone who's currently sipping Lucozade in a darkened room with a basin by their side. They can't even remember how they got home.

So if we've known about hangovers for so long, how come we've never figured out how to put a stop to them? Well, you might be surprised to hear that we *have*. A great deal of research has gone into the mystery of the hangover. People are out there every night researching themselves legless in bars, pubs and clubs all over the country. They try different combinations of drinks: wine before beer then whisky; beer before wine then whisky; vodka before beer and then wine before whisky; drinking standing up; drinking sitting down; eating before the drinking; eating during the drinking; eating after the drinking; wine before sitting down; vodka during the whisky and standing up eating in the beer (the researcher's notes get a bit confused here).

The point is, we know what causes hangovers – the Devil. He's trying to suck out your soul through your toilet and starts with everything you've had to eat in the last three days. That's one theory, anyway. Another is that drinking alcohol affects the pituitary gland causing vasopressin inhibition, dehydration and a toxic accumulation of acetaldehyde when the liver's production of glutathione is exhausted.

The scientists have all the answers and their ultimate solution to the hangover problem is . . . don't drink. But that's just crazy talk, so maybe they're not so clever after all.

There are plenty of hangover 'cures' – from Prairie Oysters and Bloody Marys to burnt toast, fried breakfasts and bananas – but only a few of them do any good at all and some of them can actually do more harm than good . . . banging yourself on the head with a dustbin lid, for example, or turning up for work. Some of the most reliable, tried and tested, traditional hangover cures are listed in this book as 'Sure Cures'. There is no guarantee, of course, that any of them will work for *you*, but some might. You might even like to try combinations of cures – a Bloody Mary goes rather well with a fried breakfast, for example, assuming that you are brave enough, and that the debilitating effect of your hangover has not left you too weak to lift the frying pan. Having a wife, husband, partner or significant other on hand is the best idea; then, all you have to concentrate on is not passing out or throwing up when it's put in front of you.

Different cures, obviously, will work better or worse for different people – the trick is knowing which one works best for you, and you can really only come to terms with that through trial and error. Be warned that the trials can be really trying, and the errors can be very, very messy. To guide you through these tough choices, *The Hangover Companion* gives a fair and unbiased assessment of each of the 'Sure Cures'.

If you need cheering up more than resuscitation, they do say that laughter is the best medicine. This is a tricky one. 'They' have obviously never had the headache from hell that makes a hiccup sound like Krakatoa. When you're suffering with a head like that, the last thing you want is a belly laugh echoing around in there but just in case it might work for you, there are liberal doses of 'The Best Medicine' jokes scattered throughout this hangover handbook.

If you need something to take your mind off your suffering, then have a look at the 'Strange But True' stories. If nothing else, they will usually help to reassure you that there are undoubtedly others worse off than yourself, something from which you can always draw the inspiration needed to set you off on the rocky road to recovery.

To provide further distraction there are also a few wise words quoted from drinkers who really should have known better, plenty of hard facts about booze that will either serve to warn you off or leave you smacking your lips ready to tackle a 'hair of the dog', and far more information than any hangover sufferer could ever be expected to absorb in one sitting, even if that sitting is spent locked in the smallest room in the house for safety reasons.

You have in your hands the best possible way to help you endure the rigours of your hungover day, so prop open your eyelids, set your thumbs to flicking through the pages, and enjoy a good read.

If all be true that I do think,
There are five reasons we should drink;
Good wine — a friend — or being dry —
Or lest we should be by and by —
Or any other reason why.

HENRY ALDRICH

Part 1
Genesis Of The Hangover

There are all sorts of reasons why people like to have a good drink. Everyone enjoys celebrating landmark events like weddings, birthdays, Christmas, a promotion, your team winning or a new baby. You might feel like having a drink just because you've got a new job, you're in love, your mum's won the lottery, your dog's had puppies – or if your job sucks, you've been dumped, your mum's been rushed to hospital with a heart attack and the ambulance flattened your dog into a road rug. Hell, why not just get drunk?

Therein lies the problem – there are so many good reasons to have a drink or two – reasons small and large. Whether you've just heard that someone in the office next door has got new shoes ('Hurrah! Let's have a drink!') or whether you've just heard that your cancer's in remission ('Yippee! Let's have a drink and a smoke!'), you will use it as an excuse to get a few down your neck. Some of us just like to celebrate lunchtime coming round each day. And why not? Well, drinking too much really isn't good for you, as we all know, and every drink you take takes you one step closer to the dreaded hangover.

Everything you do the night before the morning after contributes in some way towards the type of hangover that lies in store for you – especially the drinking, of course. Different kinds of drink will engender different styles of hangover on different types of people, but a major factor in the depth and breadth of your hangover is how you behaved while achieving it. Heavy guilt at having confided in your best friend's girlfriend that he's only seeing her because she has fabulous knockers and her sister wouldn't have him will turn that dark cloud in your head into a thunderstorm the moment you remember what you said. The early-morning phone call from your former best friend will probably serve as a reminder. Deep regret over having disgraced yourself by spraying a fountain of beer over a funeral party, squeezing portions of the landlord's wife that are no-go areas even for the landlord, or convincing yourself that the entire bar will be hugely amused to see you display your genitals inside a pint glass, will send you straight to the bottom of the darkest, loneliest hangover pit in history.

To some extent, women expect that men will behave progressively worse the more they drink. After one or two, most men can be charming, even humorous. After three or four, a man's intentions tend to become a little too obvious. Thereafter, his subtlety usually deserts him completely, slamming the door on the way out. Women, of course, know that the main difference between man and a pig is that pigs don't turn into men when they drink.

Behaving like a pig will, undoubtedly, make you feel like something from the farmyard the next morning – perhaps something you would rather not have trodden in, or perhaps one of the lowly creatures that scratches around on the ground. You may, for example, look a bit like a chicken when you discover that you can focus better if you stare at things with one eye at a time; you may walk around like a duck with piles, moan like a cow in labour and, to complete the farmyard effect, produce a stench of the right volume and texture.

Little wonder, then, that many women would rather have a drink with their friends than have sex. With a drink, after all, size doesn't really matter and you can still enjoy a soft one. But should that innocent couple of drinks with the girls get out of hand, women suffer hangovers far worse than men. That feeling of disgrace or regret that makes a man's hangover feel so much worse is infinitely more acute for a lady who may have lost her dignity the night before. Men who remain sober enough to realize that women are behaving badly are overcome with a primeval predatory instinct. At first, they view women who are drinking as being fun; after another two or three drinks they see them as a definite opportunity, then they simply become a burden. Try loading a girl into a taxi when she's just gone over the edge and turned from being a sex bomb into a sack of slinkies.

By the time you have turned into a rubber man or woman, however, (having pulled on your cloak of indestructibility that allows you to bounce off walls, pavements and buses to no apparent ill effect), it is too late to start worrying about the hangover that's going to happen at home the next morning. Your concerns will be far more immediate. You need to worry about things like, 'How the hell do I get home?', 'Where do I live?', 'How can a lamp post jump out at me like that?' and 'Who put this flowerbed in my face?'

How can a few drinks turn you from being a fully-functioning, responsible adult into an uncoordinated moron who blunders around like a Cyberman with a common-sense short circuit? The truth is that alcohol, while generally acting as a depressant, can simultaneously act as a stimulant, such are its miracle properties. Once alcohol is in your bloodstream, it is able to cross what is referred to as the 'blood-brain barrier' that filters so many other potential toxins, and thereby stimulate the cortex, hippocampus and nucleus accumbens. These areas of the brain are responsible for reasoning and pleasure. Once that happens you are really in trouble because alcohol interference in those parts of the brain obviously makes you think, 'That was bloody marvellous. Give me more.' The alcohol in your brain also causes relaxation, possibly by stimulating the production of alpha waves in the brain that are associated with enjoyment.

So, basically, the booze has invaded your brain and told you you're having a good time. It has acted as a stimulant in some areas of your brain, encouraging you to drink more. Unfortunately, this will then begin to act as a depressant, affecting other brain functions. Certain areas of your brain are subdued, causing a lowering of inhibitions. That's what made you think your nuts and todger would look so good under glass. The alcohol will also slow down your thought processes, including those that control memory, memory, memory and . . . I can't remember what else. This slowing of the brain dulls your senses and reduces your overall reaction time. It now takes you far longer for your brain to process all the sensory data being fed into it – sight, hearing, smell, taste and touch – and to figure out what's going on around you. Your motor functions will be impaired. The instant it took your brain to realize that your legs were heading in the wrong direction was an instant too long, which is why you ended up propping up the pansies in the flower bed.

Alcohol also impairs the processing of glucose in the occipital lobe. This is the bit of your grey matter that controls your sight, and the effect of alcohol blurs your vision. As well as all of this, alcohol in your bloodstream can cause a distortion in the shape of your cupola. Before you start checking your trousers, it's in your ear. The little blobby cupola brushes against fibres inside your ear to send nerve impulses to your brain that control your balance. Needless to say, that's all shot to pieces and this is one of the most significant factors in creating the hangover from hell.

The Best Medicine

Sister Josephine, one of the nuns who taught at a girls-only convent school, was asked to bring her most trustworthy pupil to the Mother Superior's office one day. The Mother Superior, a shy and unworldly woman, struggled to make her wishes known.

'Take this money,' she said to the student, 'and go to the local chemist where I want you to get me . . . ummm . . . something to help with my . . . er . . . ' she whispered, '. . . constipation.'

'Oh, I couldn't,' said the young girl. 'I – I don't think I could ask at the counter for such a thing.'

'Don't worry,' said Sister Josephine. 'I will pop down to the shops myself. It's almost lunchtime, anyway.'

Instead of taking the money to the chemist, however, Sister Josephine took it to the off-licence and bought a half-bottle of whisky. By the time she got back to the school she was well sozzled – singing, dancing and belching her way across the schoolyard.

'Sister Josephine!' gasped the young girl. 'You were supposed to use that money to buy something for the Mother Superior's . . . um . . . problem.'

'I did!' screeched Sister Josephine. 'When she sees the state of me, she's going to fucking shit herself!'

Sure Cure

BLOODY MARY

One of the finest hair-of-the-dog hangover cures known to man (or beast, if that's how you happen to be feeling), everyone who has ever tried a Bloody Mary will tell you a different way of making one. Some like to add a spoonful of horseradish, more pepper or even more vodka, and different variations can be made using gin or tequila. You need to try a few to get it just the way you like it. Try a few too many, of course, and you'll be right back where you started!

> 1 measure vodka
> 3 measures tomato juice
> $2/3$ measure lemon juice
> Large splosh of Worcestershire sauce
> Large splosh of Tabasco sauce
> 1 pinch of black pepper
> 1 pinch of celery salt
> 1 slice of lemon or lime
> 1 stick of celery

Mix everything together in a big glass and serve over ice with a slice of lime or lemon and a stick of celery.

Aardvark

Well, what's an A to Z without an aardvark? It has very little relevance to your hangover unless you happen to be Swedish, in which case it is a good idea to stay home from the office and avoid any aard vark.

Aliens

You will not remember, when you wake up, how the thing in the bed beside you came to be there. She, or he, may not be your type. He, or she, may not even appear to be the same species. Try to stay cool and remember that she or he is probably thinking exactly the same about you.

Ang-naff-nang

No one knows what the hell it means, but it is the first thing most hungover drunks say when they wake up. May be linked to tongue swelling (see *Tongue*) and dental problems (see *Teeth*). May also be a village in deepest Cambodia, but how would anyone with a hangover know that unless they had been given a mystical message when in a trance-like sleep about the jungle village where the miracle hangover cure can be found? (See *Jungle*.)

Arse Acne

The effects of a hangover down under and the consequent scrubbing can leave your arse with a rash of spots. Mind you, a hangover can do the same to your face, so you might want to choose which looks best, wear your trousers on your head, walk on your hands and teach your bum to talk.

Arsehole

It's the thing that causes most problems to hungover curry addicts. It's the thing that you made of yourself when you dominated the karaoke machine last night. You may now also feel so embarrassed that it's the thing you want to pull over your head to make you disappear.

Aspirin

Traditional pain-relief remedy which, like so many others, should only be contemplated if you feel strong enough to cope with that horrendous fizzing noise.

*I neither drink nor smoke
and am
a hundred per cent fit.*

FIELD MARSHAL MONTGOMERY

*I drink and smoke
and I am
two hundred per cent fit!*

WINSTON CHURCHILL

Strange But True . . .

In Settler, Canada, an eighteen-year-old driver, David Zurfluh, was pulled over by the police after his car was seen weaving about on the road. The officers naturally suspected that Zurfluh had been drinking and they weren't wrong. As soon as his car stopped he was out the door, running away unsteadily in various directions and nowhere near as fast as he thought he was going. It wasn't too difficult, on this occasion, for the Mounties to get their man. In the back of the police car, however, Zurfluh came up with a novel way of fooling the breathalyzer. Before the officers could stop him, he tore the crotch out of his underpants, stuffed the material in his mouth and started to eat it. He believed that the cotton fabric would absorb the alcohol and give a negative breath-test reading – and it worked! According to the breathalyzer he was within the legal limit. They charged him anyway, but he was later acquitted in court.

Blame It All On The Booze

BEER

If your latest hangover from hell is the result of having a few too many beers in the pub last night, don't blame yourself, don't blame the landlord and don't blame the brewer – blame the Sumerians. No, they are not a race of evil bodysnatchers from outer space who are trying to invade your head. The Sumerians lived in Mesopotamia, which lay in the region around the Tigris and Euphrates rivers, an area that is now part of Iraq, Kuwait and northern Saudi Arabia. Often referred to as the 'cradle of civilization', it was here that the Sumerians established the first major cities, developing ways of counting and the first known forms of writing. One Sumerian pictogram from around 3000 BC shows the world's first written recipe – not for bread or fish fingers or pot noodles, but for beer.

It's impossible to say which particular Sumerian is actually responsible for your hangover because nobody knows who invented beer. It's highly unlikely that a Sumerian genius sitting in the sun on a hot day suddenly thought, 'Man, I'm gagging for a pint. I think I'll invent beer.' One theory is that the fermentation process was discovered by accident when grain-based porridge or gruel started fermenting all on its own in the sunshine. Someone must have been brave enough to taste it, got mildly pissed and decided he liked it.

The fermentation process was refined over the centuries and the practice of drinking beer, which would have been highly nutritious and was part of the staple diet of many cultures, quickly spread. In ancient Egypt, stonemasons were paid in kash. No, that hasn't been misspelt and it wasn't a tradesman's way of dodging the tax man. Kash was a kind of beer and the word 'cash' is thought to come from the ancient tradition of paying in kash.

Sadly for the ancient Egyptians, they'd have to wait several thousand years if they wanted a bag of crisps or scampi fries with their beer. They wouldn't have to wait quite so long if they fancied a lager. The amber nectar came along in the sixteenth century. Lager is fermented in a different way to other beers, being produced in a cooler environment with yeast that sinks to the bottom of the fermentation vessel rather than floating on the top. Since the process was discovered by Bavarian monks almost 500 years ago, lager has gone on to become the world's most widely drunk beer. Altogether, world production of beer stands at around 1,500 million hectolitres (a hectolitre is 100 litres) a year. If you popped out to the pub every night and drank ten pints, you could polish off twelve months' world output in just 72 million years. The hangover you would have after a binge like that would be of truly epic proportion.

A TO Z OF HANGOVERS B

Barf

A barf is an alarming type of puke that takes you almost by surprise. If you have managed to make it to a toilet, have a bucket handy or get your girlfriend's handbag open in time, it is all over remarkably quickly. The 'b' sound at the beginning of the word denotes a reluctant withholding of the torrent, the 'ar' shows that this is a high-volume puke delivered at some velocity with the mouth wide open. The 'f' is just tidying up.

Birlies

If you have 'the birlies' you can tell straight away that you are going to wake up with a hangover. The term comes from a Scots word 'birl', which means to spin or whirl and describes that feeling you get when you lie on your bed and the whole room starts revolving at great speed. If you're lucky, the feeling will pass after what seems like several years but is actually only a few seconds. But when were you ever that lucky? Keep a basin handy.

Boak

This is a kind of hearty, baritone barf (see *Barf*). It tends to last for longer and comes from deep within, somewhere down around the knees. As such it can achieve great distance on expulsion, allowing a practiced boaker to stand on one side of the road and puke on the opposite pavement. For most, however, the boak is a draining, exhausting experience.

Brain Splitting

Surprisingly, considering that it is 83 per cent water, the brain doesn't really mix well with whisky. A pounding in the brain is a typical hangover symptom. One theory for its cause is that alcohol causes the brain to divide. Just as you reach your critical consumption level, you develop two brains, one saying, 'I think you've had enough now,' and the other saying, 'Bollocks! You can drink all night!' Then they start to fight and they're still beating the crap out of each other when you wake up in the morning.

Breath

The stinky cloud that comes out of your mouth. Worse with smokers and curry lovers, who can wilt flower displays at ten paces – even plastic ones.

Breathe

Don't forget to.

Bum

Your bum can suffer terribly during a hangover and needs to be treated with kid gloves – not literally, that's just kinky – but with the utmost of care. Look after your bum and your bum will never let you down. Actually, it will let you down, of course, and let you stand up again, that's the whole point of a bum. Not that you have a point to your bum unless you're some kind of freak – bums are round – but you rely on your bum far more than you would ever think. After all, without your bum, you'd have nothing to fall back on. Take good care of it (see *Wipes*).

The Best Medicine

Following Sister Josephine's disgraceful performance (see page 16), the Mother Superior decides to demonstrate the evils of drink during a science class.

'Watch closely, girls,' she said, placing two glasses on the table, one containing a clear liquid and the other a golden liquid. She then held up a wriggling worm in each hand. 'I will now place this live worm in a glass of water.'

The worm continued to wriggle, none the worse for its immersion in the water.

'Now,' said the Mother Superior, 'I will place the other worm in a glass of whisky.'

She lowered the worm into the golden liquid, whereupon it went as stiff as a nail and sank to the bottom, dead.

'So,' she said, gravely, 'what does this experiment prove?'

'It's obvious,' said a girl near the front. 'Drink plenty of whisky if you've got worms.'

Sure Cure

PRAIRIE OYSTER

Warning: read no further if you are feeling a bit queasy. The real Prairie Oyster (or Rocky Mountain Oyster) is a bollock. Out on the range, cowpokes fry them up for breakfast after the calves, have been castrated. This takes a bit of getting used to, especially for the calves, and it has something in common with the Prairie Oyster drink in that respect. Variations on the drink will have a spoonful of ketchup, olive oil or vinegar added, or may use only the yolk of the egg, but the basic Prairie Oyster is:

> 1 whole raw egg
> 1 dash of Worcestershire sauce
> 1 pinch of salt
> 1 pinch of pepper

Gently crack the egg into a glass, add the Worcestershire sauce and seasoning, give it a gentle swirl without breaking the yolk and swallow the whole lot in one.

Not for the faint-hearted, pregnant women, elderly people or faint-hearted, pregnant, elderly people.

HANGOVERS IN HISTORY

Turkey, 2000 BC (approx.)

Man, that was a hell of a party last night.

Tell me about it. I never knew there was that much wine in the whole world.

There isn't now.

Why didn't you let me go home when I'd had enough?

We were in your house.

Still, it was good to see the Greeks leave. They never know when they've outstayed their welcome.

They were never exactly welcome – and ten years is a long time to stay. Great booze-up, though.

Gaaaa . . . now my tongue's so dry I feel like I've got one of your sandals in my mouth.

I wondered where it had gone.

How come we had to do the first stint of guard duty?

Probably something to do with me calling the captain a dozy pillock and you calling the sergeant a big fat poof.

I didn't, did I? Oh, noooo . . . I did! But . . . but normally that would mean us being stoned!

We were . . . totally.

No, I mean stoned to death by people chucking rocks.

Well, the captain had passed out and the sergeant was snogging the corporal so there was nobody left to organize a proper stoning.

My arms feel like lead. I can hardly lift my spear.

Mine are the same. I bet everyone else is like that, too. Another good reason for not stoning us – nobody's got the strength to lift a decent-sized rock.

It was hauling on those ropes that did it, wasn't it?

You're right there – and what on earth was the point? I mean, open your eyes and look at that thing. We had to haul that all the way up from the beach. I didn't think we'd get it through the gates.

Me neither. And just what does the city of Troy need with a bloody great wooden horse anyway?

I dunno. Hang on a minute . . . there's a little door opened in its belly. You know, I think there's someone inside . . .

Chicken Ringstinger

This is the curry your mates dared you to order and said you were too chicken to eat; curries like a Madras, a Vindaloo or the daddy of them all, the Phal. No matter how hot they are when you eat them, they are guaranteed to feel ten times hotter when they come thundering out the other end at 3.00 a.m. Not only does this truly volcanic activity make your arsehole feel like the rim of Mount Vesuvius, but prolonged confinement on the crapper leaves your legs so weak that they offer about as much support as two sticks of overboiled asparagus. Don't take the dare.

Chin

Hangover injuries to the chin are commonplace and can include the imprint from the engagement ring of the girl in the nightclub whose left hook finally persuaded you that she was actually spoken for; grazing (see

Friction Burns, Elbows, Knees and *Forehead*); and a slobber rash from when you were licking the pub table in an attempt to prove that, like fingerprints, no two people have the same tongue print.

Chunder

Means 'vomit' (noun) or 'to vomit' (verb) . . . but the sound of the word, like a cross between 'thunder' and 'chutney', implies lots of noise and lumpy bits.

Coffee

Drinking strong, black coffee will not cure your hangover but it is a stimulant, so it will wake you up enough to fully appreciate how crap you feel. Because caffeine is a vasoconstrictor it could help to reduce the size of the swollen blood vessels that are giving you such a headache. It is also, however, a diuretic; this will make you want to pee, leaving you dehydrated – which can provoke headaches. All-in-all a cup of coffee's a bit of a double-edged sword, really.

Crap

A handy, catch-all term, easy to pronounce for the verbally challenged hangover sufferer, that describes in a nutshell the way you look, the way you are feeling, your recent behaviour and the mess in your pants.

Strange But True . . .

Even seasoned, semi-professional drinkers will sometimes experience strange cravings when they've had a couple too many, which is why foodstuffs like chips in curry sauce, pork scratchings and pickled eggs were invented. Those with a sweet tooth might opt for chocolate, cake or even chocolate cake, but in 2003 a sixty-year-old man in Escobedo, Mexico, decided that he wanted honey. Having drunk himself almost to a standstill, he reasoned that the best place to find honey was in a beehive and he happened to know exactly where to find such a thing. The bees, of course, were none too happy about the drunk attempting to break into their nest to steal their honey and attacked him. Over a thousand bees swarmed all over the man, stinging him mercilessly. He then went into anaphylactic shock and died.

It wouldn't have happened with a pickled egg.

*More people get
out of your way if
you say, 'I'm going
to puke!' then if you
say, 'Excuse me.'*

SALLY BERGER

The Best Medicine

A man stumbles down to breakfast determined to try to force some food inside him in the hope that it will cure his abominable hangover. His wife happily flits around the kitchen rustling up some bacon and eggs, toast and coffee, chatting all the while.

'So what do you think?' she asks.

'About what?' he groans, sipping his coffee.

'Do you think I'm still in good shape?' she twittered. 'Personally, I think I could have a better figure if I had breast enlargement surgery, don't you?'

'You don't need surgery for that,' grumbled her husband. 'Just rub toilet paper between them for a while.'

'What are you talking about?' she frowned. 'Will that make them bigger?'

'Dunno,' said the man, 'but it worked for your arse.'

Sure Cure

HAIR OF THE DOG

Similia similibus curantura sounds like just the sort of gibberish you and your mates were talking last night but will not be an expression familiar to you unless you happen to be a Latin scholar. It basically means 'like cures like' and dates back to Roman times when they believed this to be the case. Although they may have found it difficult to persuade some poor Christian who'd just had his leg chewed off by a lion in the arena that offering the lion his other leg was the answer to all his problems.

The idea persisted, however, and at one time people believed that if they were bitten by a mad dog, they should pluck a hair from the tail of the dog (presumably this would make it *really* mad) and burn it. The hair, that is, not the dog. Burning the dog would make it as mad as hell. You then either crushed the hair into a drink, ate it or placed it inside the wound to avoid catching rabies.

Nowadays, to have a 'hair of the dog that bit you' means to go back down to the pub, completely ignoring any dogs you may see on the way, and have some more of what you had last night to cure your hangover. This does not, of course, cure your hangover at all, but once you get past the first couple of drinks you won't much care any more.

Daylight

This is something that happens every morning, unless you are lucky enough to live inside the Arctic Circle where you can go for months during the winter without having the trauma of being woken by it at all. For most hangover sufferers, however, it's something you just have to live with, unless you can sleep right through till night-time or have mastered the art of walking around with your eyes shut. Keep a pair of sunglasses by your bed (see *Sunglasses*) to combat the worst effects.

Diarrhoea

It's a tricky word to spell, especially as it's usually pronounced 'Yiiiiiiiiiiiiiiiiiiiiiiiiiiiiii!!!!' Take a note of it so you can write it on a scrap of paper to slide across the counter in the pharmacy.

Death

Sometimes this is the best you can hope for.

Delirium Tremens

Known as the DTs for short. You might feel a bit jittery and trembly with your hangover, but if you've got the DTs then you're really in trouble. Uncontrollable shaking and hallucinating, by seeing snakes, rats or giant insects, are a few of the symptoms. This usually only affects alcoholics, so before you go screaming for an ambulance after seeing a seven-legged creature, make sure it wasn't just the dog with his lead in his mouth.

Dopeler Effect

This is the hangover phenomenon that makes incredibly stupid concepts seem like good ideas. Getting out of bed, turning up the radio, bending over to tie your laces or setting off for work all fall into this category.

Dribbling

Keep a tissue handy to dab at the dribble that may froth from the side of your mouth, and check your pulse from time to time to make sure you're not having a stroke.

Drink

Drink lots for a hangover. Yes, of course, that's how you got into this mess in the first place, but when you have a hangover you have to drink lots of water – not booze – to rehydrate yourself. Dehydration causes headaches (see *Brain Splitting*), so drink as much water as you can bear. You can argue that beer is mainly water, but that's the sort of attitude that's going to leave you unshaven, flea-bitten and foul-smelling, sitting on an old great-coat (only homeless drunks know where to find these coats) begging for enough to buy your next can of super lager. By that stage, your recovery is going to require more than just a couple of bottles of Evian.

Drugs

Just say no.

HANGOVERS IN HISTORY

Valley of Elah, Israel, eleventh century BC

Come on, mate, you've got to get up.

Go hump a camel.

No, really . . . they're expecting you.

Expecting me to do what . . . throw up?

It's not as though you had that much last night.

Had more than you.

You always have more than me.

No, I meant all five hundred of you.

Oh, yeah – you won the speed-drinking contest.

Yup, beat everyone in turn – losers.

Just as well we didn't invite the rest of the lads, really.

Why? You think I could feel any worse?

You could try taking that wet cloth off your face and stand up.

Only if you've stopped the world spinning.

We could go for a walk.

You got a death wish or something?

Can I give you something for your head?

If I could unscrew it, you could have it for free.

Sounds bad. Your eyes looked bloodshot, too.

You should see them from this side.

The boss is going to be pretty pissed off if you don't show up.

He doesn't need me. He can fight his own battles.

No, actually, that's exactly what he does need you for.

Okay . . . hand me my sword and help me up.

Ataboy! It's only some kid called David. It'll all be over in seconds, Goliath, no worries . . .

Blame It All On The Booze

WINE

It's a pretty safe bet that the world's first ever hangover was caused not by beer or whisky or vodka or alcopops, but by wine. People have been drinking wine for longer than any other kind of booze and traces of some kind of wine, thought to have been made either from hawthorn berries or grapes, have been found on pieces of Chinese pottery dating back more than 9,000 years. One American archaeologist has even analyzed wine that had been sealed in bronze flasks for more than 3,000 years. It smelled of flowers and had a herb or flower flavouring. Another archaeological find came at Hajji Firuz Tepe, in the mountains of Iran, where a 9-litre wine container was unearthed. It's a lot easier to pop down to Sainsbury's for your plonk.

Just as beer was probably first produced by accident, spoiled grapes left in a bowl may well have fermented in the sun and rendered unconscious the person who first tasted them, thus creating the world's first wino. His first words on waking were, 'Can you spare ten pence for a cuppa tea, Guv?' Given that people had been fermenting wine long before beer was discovered, the winemakers may also have had a hand in the development of ale. By the time the ancient Egyptians were sampling the odd snifter, wine had become big business, with wine traders regulated by law and thousands of casks being transported on wine barges – potentially the world's first booze cruises.

Even though the Europeans came to lay claim to being the heartland of the world wine industry, European production didn't really take off until 4,000 years after the Egyptians had started dabbling in it. Nevertheless, the world's oldest wine business still in production is believed to be the Château de Goulaine, run by the French family that has owned it for over 1,000 years. An Italian concern run by the Ricasoli family has been involved in wine and olive oil production since 1141 and is believed to have first developed Chianti.

Wine isn't only produced from grapes and fruit, of course. Some of the earliest Chinese wine was made, unsurprisingly, from rice and rice wine is still produced today. The Chinese also make wine from fish, but that's just plain loopy. It's doubtful if even the most delightful of fish vintages could compete with the world's most sought-after wines.

Annual world wine production hovers around the 7-billion-gallon mark – enough to fill more than 10,000 Olympic swimming pools. That would certainly make synchronized swimming more fun to watch, but the wine would be fairly undrinkable when you consider what people do in swimming pools. For a decent bottle of plonk what you really need to do is spend a bit of cash. Perhaps the most expensive bottle of wine ever was once owned by American President Thomas Jefferson – a 1787 Margaux that was priced at $500,000 and then broken by a clumsy waiter. The asking price for the wine was due to its value as an antique and it would not have been fit to drink, although you can bet somebody had a stinker of a hangover the next morning!

Elbows

Painful grazing on the elbows can be caused by your mates having to drag you home along the pavement by your collar. Look for fluff in the wounds (see *Knees*, *Nose*, *Forehead* and *Friction Burns*).

Elephant's Trunk

Rhyming slang for what you were last night.

Epping Hunt

Rhyming slang for what you made of yourself last night.

Extra Fit

Definitely not how you feel this morning, but rhyming slang for it nonetheless.

Ewok

For at least five minutes after you wake up, any voices you hear will sound like these furry little creatures from *Star Wars*.

Exercise

It may raise your metabolic rate, force more oxygen into your system and have all sorts of other beneficial effects, but if you're in no fit state to drive a vehicle, what makes you think that you have the coordination to work out at the gym, ride a bike or even go for a run in the park without putting both yourself and anyone you might come across (or throw up on) in mortal danger? Be sensible, stay home, watch an ancient movie on TV and have a cup of tea instead.

Exorcism

Something of a last resort, really, but if your hangover has persisted for more than thirty-six hours, you are speaking in tongues and your head is revolving through 360 degrees, it may be worth considering.

Eyeballs

It may well feel like your two brains (see *Brain Splitting*) are using your eyeballs either as punchbags or bongo drums. Resist the temptation to alleviate the pain by scooping them out with a teaspoon. The pain will subside and you should always remember that pain like this is nature's way of telling you you're a twat.

The Best Medicine

A Scotsman on holiday in Australia gets into a drinking contest in a bar with some locals, wins hands down and has to be carried back to his hotel. The next day he goes back to the bar for a hair of the dog and spots a sign on the wall that says: 'Free whisky for anyone who can pass the test.'

'I never noticed that last night,' he says.

'I'm not surprised,' says the barman. 'You were pretty drunk.'

'What's this test all about, then?' asks the Scotsman.

'You have to drink this gallon of rum with chilli peppers,' says the barman, 'without throwing up. Then we've got a crocodile outside with toothache, so you've got to pull the tooth with your bare hands. Finally, there's a woman upstairs who's never had an orgasm.'

The Scotsman has a few beers, then can resist the challenge no longer. He downs the gallon of rum and, sweating profusely from the scorching heat of the chillies and swaying unsteadily, heads outside to tackle the crocodile. A few minutes later he lurches back in, covered in cuts and with his clothes in tatters.

'That'sh him sheen to!' he slurs. 'Now where'sh the woman with the toothache?'

Sure Cure

COLD CARROT

It's a bit like cold turkey, except without the turkey. Well, no one ever looked forward to watching a carrot being carved for Christmas lunch, did they? Not even Tiny Tim. There is no alcohol involved, however, but carrots are packed with beta-carotene which your body converts into Vitamin A – and anyone with a hangover needs to up their vitamin intake. If this tasty carrot drink takes your fancy, however, beware. You need to use a blender and the noise of a blender in full flurry does not go well with a headache.

> 200 g (7 oz) of carrots
> 1 apple or 1 pear
> 1 small piece of root ginger – 1 cm ($^1/_2$ inch)

Chop the tops and bottoms off of the carrots and either scrub them or give them a scrape with a potato peeler. Peel the apple or pear and chop it up, discarding the seeds. Chop up the ginger and then give it all a whizz in the blender.

Pour it into a large glass with ice.

Five-Fingered Spread

If you are feeling nauseous, keep a bucket or basin handy. Never try to hold back the rising tide of vomit by putting your hand over your mouth. This will simply fan the puke out into a far-from-lovely fountain that will coat every horizontal or vertical surface within twenty feet. Also, remember that a sneeze leaves your nose at around 600 mph. If you seal your mouth, two chunder jets exiting your nostrils at that sort of velocity could send you backwards straight out the window.

Flatulence

An inevitable by-product of beer and curry, most hangover sufferers experience more than their normal output on the morning after. This can be very unpleasant for anyone unlucky enough to be in close proximity to you, especially in an enclosed space. Try to keep it under control, but if you must let one rip, beware the follow-through.

Floor

Your new best friend. You probably slept with it last night. You know your hangover is easing up a little (see *Peak*) when you feel you can safely lie on the floor without holding on.

Food

No matter how difficult it is to force it past the bear cub (see *Throat*) you must eat something. You need to eat to restore your blood-sugar level, replace vital minerals and fill the void left when you pebble-dashed the newsagent's window last night due to the unexpected reappearance of your curry and everything else you ate yesterday.

Forehead

Once you have made it to the bathroom, managed to focus on the thing in the mirror and have come through the denial phase (it *is* you and you know it), check your forehead for phone numbers written in lipstick or biro. Don't immediately think you must have got lucky and that someone gave you their number. It could be your own phone number in case you got lost. Anyone phoning it would find that you weren't in but your answering machine would at least be able to give them your name and paramedics like to have a name when they're trying to revive someone. Alternatively, it could be the number of the local Samaritans; if it has been written backwards this shows true consideration as it allows you to read it in the mirror. Also check for strange abrasions (see *Friction Burns*, *Chin*, *Knees* and *Elbows*).

Friction Burns

Among your many other hangover aches and pains, you may find seemingly inexplicable grazes or burns on your elbows, knees, forehead, chin and nose. If you can bear to take a closer look, *CSI*-style, you might find familiar carpet fibres embedded in these wounds. You may well congratulate yourself, mistakenly believing that you got lucky on the rug. But how likely is that, really? You almost certainly fell flat on your face having arrived home naked (see *Nudity*).

***March is the month that God designed to show those who don't drink what a hangover's like.**

GARRISON KEILLOR*

Strange But True . . .

The morning after a gallon or two of beer and a mighty vindaloo, eruptions in the trouser department are inevitable. This can be pretty disgusting for anyone sitting next to you on the bus or for anyone who has to share an office with you, although you will undoubtedly find the aroma far less offensive than they will. Most people happily tolerate the smell of their own farts and some positively adore it, even if they are feeling a bit worse for wear. For one unfortunate man in the Netherlands in 2003, however, the guffs emitted by his friends proved to be his downfall. His 'friends' were the dozens of parrots he kept in his double-glazed house where he allowed them to fly free. The parrot-fart gas coupled with the ammonia from their droppings built up in the poorly ventilated premises until it began to make him feel unwell. He called for an ambulance before collapsing but by the time the paramedics arrived he was dead, half-suffocated and half-poisoned from inhaling parrot farts.

HANGOVERS IN HISTORY

Somewhere in Britain, sixth century AD

Do you have to make so much noise?

Well, one of us has got to do some work around here.

Sit down, you fool, you're swaying about all over the place.

No, I'm not – you just can't see straight.

You're right. I feel like a dung heap. There was something bad in that barrel of mead last night.

The only bad thing in it was your head.

I had to prove the point.

What point . . . that a man cannot drown in ale?

That's the one.

You only survived by drinking it all.

It was a close thing, though.

The serving wench at the banquet wasn't impressed.

She fancied me.

She said she'd rather kiss a donkey's arse.

She didn't mean it, though.

It was a turn of phrase . . . you didn't have to go fetch that donkey . . . or kiss its arse yourself.

The donkey didn't mind.

How do you reckon that, then?

He followed me home.

So that's how you got in to work so early. You rode the donkey here.

No, he was still asleep. I didn't like to wake him so I walked.

I'm not even going to ask what that means. You were obviously feeling better earlier on then?

Yeah, I felt fine when I got here. I even got most of the cutting done.

What? You mean that lot over there? You were still pissed – you've ruined the entire supply of that special timber!

It's cut exactly according to instructions.

But it's all curved, you idiot!

That's so we can make what he wanted – a round table to seat twenty-five men.

No, he wanted a table to seat around *twenty-five men. What's King Arthur going to do with a round table . . . ?*

A TO Z OF HANGOVERS G

Garden

Always remember that there is a huge difference between a flower bed and your own bed. Just because *you* made it indoors and didn't sleep in the garden yourself, however, doesn't mean that your best pal, just a few paces behind, was given the same option. A door slammed in your face can make a shrubbery seem the ideal place to take a kip. Check the garden in the morning for unconscious drinking buddies and plants that are swaying, singing and have the hiccups. Those are the ones you kindly 'watered' on your way in.

Genitals

The dull throbbing is there to remind you never, ever again to challenge your mates to a goolie-grabbing contest. It is not, and never has been, an Olympic sport, no matter what you may have read about the ancient Greeks.

Gestapo

There are always a couple of self-righteous teetotal twats at work who will phone to find out why you have not shown up. If you haven't woken up in time to pre-empt their call (see *Groan*), use your answering machine to check out if it's them. If you don't have an answering machine, feign death or get the dog to answer the phone.

God

Don't keep calling out to Him. He's abandoned you.

Gout

It's not just an ancient Henry VIII thing. Gout is caused by a build-up of uric acid in the bloodstream when your system is overloaded. Certain foods do it and too much booze certainly will. Not everyone suffers from gout as it is now believed to be a genetic disorder, so blame your mother.

Groan

You should practise a convincing groan – not the weepy, sobbing hungover sort of whimper – so that when you phone work to claim you have a bad back, sore throat, upset stomach or migraine (all of which you may actually have anyway) it won't sound like you are just trying to skive off with a hangover. If you were drinking with workmates and the person who answers the phone groans back at you, you know you're not going to get away with it.

Guts

You have about 7.5 metres (25 feet) of gut inside you. Every single millimetre may well feel like it is on fire, attempting to tie itself in enough knots to win a boy-scout merit badge, trying to escape through your arsehole, or all three. There are plenty of remedies for an upset stomach available from your local pharmacist. There are none in your bathroom cabinet. Why didn't you buy some?

Blame It All On The Booze

WHISKY

A whisky hangover is one of the foulest, foggiest head-thumpers you can ever have the misfortune to experience. If you enjoy drinking whisky, of course, it's the price you have to pay for enjoying yourself that little bit too much. Some say that whisky is 'an acquired taste' – a drink that you have to try very hard to like. If that's the case, then countless millions of drinkers have learned how to acquire a taste for the stuff. Scotch whisky has been around for at least 500 years and it is one of the top five export revenue earners in the UK, with over a billion bottles sold annually. The French buy more whisky in a month than they do Cognac in a year.

The kilted tipplers north of the border are not, however, the only ones to have produced whisky, although they do claim that theirs is the best. They class anything but Scotch as 'Nae guid', 'Pish' and 'Sassenach shite' but whisky has, nonetheless, also been produced in Ireland (the Irish claim to have invented it and taken their expertise with them when they settled in Scotland a thousand years ago), Wales, the Isle of Man, Canada, Germany, Japan, Australia, India, the Czech Republic, Jamaica, Palestine and America.

American Whiskey – they like to spell it with 'e', as the Irish do – is different from Scotch. It will still leave you staggering around if you drink too much and will give you a hangover that makes you feel like you've been caught in a buffalo stampede, but it does taste different.

Whiskey is made from concoctions of corn or rye rather than the barley traditionally used to make Scotch, mainly because the early American whiskey-makers couldn't grow decent barley and probably tried to spell it 'barly' just to be annoying.

Don't let anyone tell you that whisky shouldn't be drunk with mixers. While many whisky-lovers prefer their dram straight, especially if they are drinking a particularly good single malt, some very special Scotch actually benefits from adding a drop or two of spring water. Other whiskies and whiskeys make fine drinks when you add ginger ale, soda, lemonade or even Coke, although the thought of such adulteration would make most outraged Scots roar louder than all of the extras in *Braveheart* being hurled from the summit of Ben Nevis.

The word 'whisky' comes from a version of the Gaelic *uisge beatha*, meaning 'water of life', with *uisge* pronounced 'oo-iss-gee'. The weird words don't end there, though. Different brands of Scotch have been given names such as Pig's Nose, Sheep Dip, Black Cock (could be nasty) and Bunnahabhain. The latter may be Gaelic or it might just be a clever marketing ploy, given that anyone stumbling up to a bar after too much whisky is going to sound like they're asking for it.

The Best Medicine

It's easy to forget to zip up your flies when you have a hangover. Here are ten easy ways to tell your best mate that he's letting a draft in.

1. Dick Peeper is at the front desk.

2. Little Elvis has left the building.

3. Snakey says hello.

4. Is Mr President expecting Monica?

5. The chick has flown the nest.

6. Everyone thought you were mad, now they can see your nuts.

7. Did you leave the cellar door open?

8. Ready to launch the missile?

9. The lonesome cowboy's out on the range.

10. You've got Windows on your lap top.

Sure Cure

BUCK'S FIZZ

An excellent early-morning pick-me-up – as long as you don't have too many, in which case it becomes an excellent early-morning pick-me-up-off-the-floor – the Buck's Fizz combines all the goodness and nutrition of fresh orange juice with all of the effervescence of champagne. Buck's Fizz probably goes better with a refined breakfast of kedgeree than it does with sausage, bacon and eggs in a bap but it almost certainly goes best of all with another Buck's Fizz to follow. Then you're on the dangerous road that's signposted 'Back Where You Started'.

> 2 parts champagne
> 1 part orange juice

Best served in a champagne flute – a tea mug just won't do. Give it a bit of a stir and then try not to drink it too fast.

Hands

The hands of a hungover drunk take on a life all of their own, knocking over anything likely to make a mess, from a bottle of milk to a cup of coffee. A touch of the DTs (see *Delerium Tremens*) will have them shaking like butterflies on a road drill. Put the shakes to good use and whip yourself up some scrambled eggs. If the clumsiness and trembling persist, stick them in your coat pockets where they can do no harm. Don't stick them in your trouser pockets as anyone spotted in a bus queue with their hands juddering away around their crotch is liable to be arrested.

Headache

See *Brain Splitting*.

Hearing

A hangover gives you hearing more sensitive than Superman eavesdropping in a library. On no account attempt to eat crisps or cornflakes as this will sound like a battalion of stormtroopers goose-stepping into Poland.

Heave

Unlike some of the other words associated with vomiting, 'heave' doesn't necessarily sound like what it is. If it did it would be called a

'Dwooooooshit!' You will, nevertheless, become acquainted with the heave while becoming reacquainted with your dinner. A good heave will throw your shoulders forward, thrust your hips upwards and suck your tummy in like you're a ski jumper exiting the ramp. There's nothing you can do once you're committed to a whole-hearted heave, you just have to go for it. Just pray that you've something substantial to heave, otherwise you're going to feel like an orang-utan has reached down your throat in an attempt to turn you inside out. (See also *Retch*).

Hiccups

Just when you thought it was safe to rejoin the world of the living, long after many of your other hangover symptoms have subsided, you can be afflicted with the dreaded hiccups. Some of the little devils come accompanied by a foul-smelling burp – nasty. There are hundreds of supposed cures for hiccups. You can blow on your thumb like you're blowing up a balloon; stand on your head for ten seconds; say 'after-dinner mints'; jump out of a plane; scream for as long as you can (this would go well with the previous cure) or breathe in and out with your face in a paper bag. Alternatively, you could try saying the words 'Hive Hearted Ice Melted' as quickly as possible over and over again. This will not cure your hiccups but it will give everyone else a good laugh.

Horse Dung

If your clothes and hair smell of horse manure when you wake up in the morning, that will teach you not to sneak up behind a mounted policeman and shout 'Boo!'

*My head feels like
there's a Frenchman
living in it.*

EDMUND BLACKADDER

Part 2
Dawn Of The Dead

The best thing to do on waking up with a hangover is not to. Stay asleep
– put it off as long as you can. Practise sleepwalking to the bathroom. Do
whatever you can to sleep it off. Failing that, you'll have to learn to deal
with it. When you first wake up, your mouth will be so dry it will feel
like a tooth-fairy vandal's been in there chalking graffiti all night.
Dehydration may seem like a strange symptom of having drunk too
much, but it is caused by the way that alcohol blocks the production of
the chemical vasopressin. There are lots of chemicals floating around
your body that are there to make your organs do their jobs properly.
Without vasopressin, your kidneys fail to help your body absorb water,
sending it to your bladder instead. You can end up pissing out four times
as much liquid as you actually consume.

So you're dried out and the first thing you need is a cup of coffee. The
coffee might help your headache, but caffeine in coffee or tea also turns
on the tap in your bladder and makes you pee, leaving you even more
dehydrated. If you're heading for the kitchen, bear in mind that you need
water or fruit juice, not just coffee.

But what's this? Suddenly the furniture is wider than you thought,
doorways have become narrower and you are blundering around like a

hippo on roller skates. You haven't been this bad at walking since you gave up wearing nappies, so what's going on? The problem is with your cupola. Remember that tiny blobby thing in your ear (see page 15) that distorted so much it ended up the size of a whale's tonsil? When you were drunk (and you should not yet be foolhardy enough to consider yourself sober), so was your cupola. It thought it would be a bit of a laugh to send messages to your brain telling it that your body was spinning. Your brain then tried to compensate for a spinning that wasn't actually happening and your eyes were dancing around, making you think that the room was going round. It was all a total cock-up and it's not over yet. While you were asleep, your brain has come to terms with the spinning and now interprets *not* spinning as spinning in the opposite direction. Take a rest, stand still, let you brain figure out where it went wrong and you will regain your balance. If you are still drunk, of course, forget it – there is no hope.

By the time you've reached the kitchen you will be feeling the full effect of the toxins that you poured down your neck last night. Some of these toxins come in the form of the congeners that are impurities produced during the fermentation process. Congeners are what give different drinks different colours and different tastes. Red wine contains more congeners than white, whisky more than vodka. Depending on your metabolism, this will mean that for some people drinking clear spirits like white rum or gin will give less of a hangover than drinking brandy or tequila. Getting the balance right is an experiment that can take years of diligent research. Toxins like congeners are responsible for the headache, the muscle ache and the stiffness in your joints, although spinning like a top and bouncing off walls the night before will also have contributed.

What you drink will affect how you feel in other ways, too. Fizzy drinks as mixers and the carbonation in beer help alcohol to be absorbed into your system more quickly, so even if you thought you were taking it easy by having a lager top or plenty of tonic with your vodka, you may just have been speeding up the rate at which you got drunk and encouraging that little demon inside your head that tells you that what you really need is just one more little drinkie . . .

If you ever find yourself in a women-versus-men battle-of-the-sexes argument, pay attention now and remember this conversation stopper. It's a scientific fact that most men have more acetaldehyde dehydrogenase and glutathione than most women. It doesn't make men better plumbers, better dentists or better drivers, but it does make them better drinkers. Acetaldehyde is a toxin that is produced when alcohol is broken down in your liver by something called alcohol dehydrogenase. Acetaldehyde dehydrogenase is then produced and it attacks the acetaldehyde along with some other stuff called glutathione. If you're reading this with a hangover, skip the long words as they will be doing your headache no good at all.

The acetaldehyde normally stands no chance and is pulverized as quickly as Frank Spencer in the ring with Mike Tyson. Sadly, the glutathione runs out quite quickly when there's a lot of alcohol swilling around. This lets more of the acetaldehyde toxin free to cause havoc in your body. Because women have less of the stuff mentioned above where the words are so long that you don't want to read them again, they don't break down the alcohol quickly enough meaning that . . . wait for it . . . they get drunk faster and have far worse hangovers!

Poor girls. Still, that's of little consolation to you if you are still feeling like a Duracell Bunny whose batteries have finally run flat. How come you feel so tired? You flopped into bed last night and were asleep before you'd made a dent in the sheets. Then you were unconscious for nearly nine hours. That surely must be more sleep than a normal person should need? Perhaps, but was it good sleep? Probably not. Could you bear another long word? Glutamine? No? Okay, let's call it glut. Glut is one of the body's home-grown stimulants. When you're having a night on the booze, the alcohol stops glut from being produced properly. You are less stimulated, so the booze makes you feel drowsy. When you stop drinking, however, your body steps up production, resulting in a . . . er, glut of glut . . . so to speak.

That means that just when you are so dog-tired that you could sleep standing up in a hammock, the glut stimulant kicks in and prevents you from falling into a proper, deep sleep. It's no wonder you're tired because you spent the night mumbling and fidgeting, reliving all those good times you had in the pub with your imagination throwing in the odd pirate duel or battle to the death with zombie flesheaters. This is one effect of what is called 'glutamine rebound' which adds to your hangover by giving you the janglies and the jitters (see page 74), feelings of anxiety and increased blood pressure. This hangover thing really messes you up, doesn't it?

The Best Medicine

God had had a pretty busy week. On the first day He created light and followed it up the next day with Heaven and the day after that with the land and all the plants. By the fourth day He was on to the stars and the planets, having realized that He needed somewhere to put all the earth and plants, and the next day He invented all of the sea creatures and birds. To cap it all, He spent the sixth day making the animals and, finally, Man. Then He sat back to celebrate, aiming to taken the seventh day off.

Waking up on the morning of the seventh day with an almighty hangover, He had one of those panicky flashback moments and thought He'd better have a quick word with Adam.

'Listen, Adam,' He said. 'I've had a bit of a rush on this week and you were the last thing on my list. I'm afraid I've got some good news and some bad news for you.'

'Okay . . . ' said Adam warily, 'so what's the good news?'

'Well,' said God, 'the good news is that I have given you a brain and a penis.'

'Great work,' said Adam, 'but what's the bad news?'

'I only gave you enough blood for you to use one at a time . . .'

Sure Cure

BLACK VELVET

If orange juice isn't quite to your taste, and, let's face it, all that acidy citrus stuff can easily disturb an already temperamental tummy, why not try an altogether smoother sensation – the Black Velvet? 'Guinness Is Good For You' is how the company's advertising slogan used to run and we all know that advertising men would never lie. To help restore vitamins and minerals, stouts like Guinness were actually given to invalids and pregnant women – pregnant men were widely believed to be faking it for a free pint – so a Black Velvet is bound to do you good.

> 1 part Guinness
> 1 part champagne

Use big parts in a big glass.

A TO Z OF HANGOVERS I

'I Don't Remember Doing/Saying That'
Don't worry, you will.

'I'm Never Drinking Again'
This is a blatant lie, none of your friends believe a word of it and you really ought to know better.

Inebriated
Badgered, banjaxed, bladdered, blasted, blathered, blitzed, blootered, blotto, clobbered, crapulous, drunk, ga-ga, goosed, guttered, hammered, jaxied, kaned, lamped, lashed, leathered, legless, mangled, mashed, merry, mullered, paralytic, pickled, piddled, pie-eyed, pished, pissed, plastered, poleaxed, potted, rat-arsed, ratted, reeling, shitfaced, sloshed, smashed, soused, sozzled, spannered, steamin', tiddly, tipsy, totalled, trashed, troused, twatted, wankered, wasted, wellied, wrecked, zombied.

Idiot
If at this stage you are struggling to recall what an idiot looks like, take a glance in the mirror. Surely only an idiot would poison himself deliberately, paying handsomely for each dose, thanking the landlord profusely for helping to administer the poison and loving every minute of the experience – until the next morning. Then there's that idiot who

stood on the table in the pub and gave everyone a rousing rendition of 'I Will Survive' while dropping lighted matches into his pants. Ah, yes . . . *now* you remember.

If Only
It is a peculiar side-effect of the hangover that you will come up with one 'If only' after another from the moment you get up, ranging from 'If only I'd come straight home from work' and 'If only I'd stayed for just one drink' to 'If only I hadn't had that curry' and 'If only I'd stayed in bed.'

Intoxication
It means 'drunkenness' but it's impossible to say when you're in the throes of it. Not to be confused with 'intaxication' – the fleeting feeling of joy you experience when you get a refund from the Inland Revenue that lasts only until you realize that it was your money to start with.

Invisibility
Sadly, all of those stupid things you got away with when you were drunk and invisible last night suddenly make your hangover ten times worse when you realize that you were not, in fact, invisible on the dance floor and you didn't get away with it at all. Start composing the apology emails now.

He that drinks fast,
pays slow.

BENJAMIN FRANKLIN

Strange But True . . .

Attila the Hun must have enjoyed a good drink. After all, when you've conquered most of Asia and spent a hard day's vanquishing, the only way to spend the evening is with a bit of a banquet and a booze-up with a few hundred of your best pillaging pals. Actually, Attila was known for taking it easy on the grog. He obviously preferred to have a clear head when he set off on the next morning's plundering but on his wedding night, in the year 453, he is said to have really cut loose and eaten far more than was good for him. His young bride, Ildico, was probably not the first and certainly not the last to have her bridegroom collapse into bed blind drunk and pass out. Her misfortune was multiplied when Attila had a massive nose bleed. Not only did this ruin the sheets, but he was too drunk to wake up, gurgling away as he slowly drowned in his own blood. Ildico was too terrified to call for help and Attila's aides were too worried about bursting in on their boss on his honeymoon night to do anything. In the morning, he was found dead in bed – one of the few guaranteed ways of avoiding a hangover.

Blame It All On The Booze

VODKA

Vodka is undoubtedly one of the world's most popular spirits. References to vodka production in Poland and Russia date back over 600 years, but the drink owes at least some of its popularity nowadays to the fact that while it is traditionally colourless some people also believe that it is odourless and can be drunk without leaving the smell of booze on your breath. Who are they kidding? There's no way that anyone who's had a skinful of vodka smells like a nun on Evian. What may be true is that it is less likely to give you the kind of hangover you can expect from some other spirits. Vodka is clear because of the way that the spirit, distilled from grain in much the same way that whisky is made (although it can also be made from potatoes, soybeans, grapes or a number of other natural sources of starch and sugar), is filtered through charcoal to remove the congeners and other impurities. Keeping the spirit pure and free of toxins helps to reduce the hangover effect and that alone is enough to make it enormously popular.

In the mid-seventies vodka took over from whisky as the most widely consumed spirit in America, despite the fact that it was invented by those pesky Ruskie commies. Of course, it helped that it became 'cool' to be seen drinking vodka. One of the coolest dudes on the planet, James Bond, was noted for ordering the vodka martini – famously 'shaken not shtirred'. The recipe for his favourite tipple appeared in the novel *Casino*

Royale where it was described as three measures of gin, one measure of vodka and half a measure of an aperitif called Kina Lillet. The vodka martini is also called the 'vodkatini' but Bond would never be so uncool as to ask for something that sounded as girly as that.

Adding mixers and creating cocktails with vodka – always a popular move because of its neutral taste – somewhat cancels out any anti-hangover properties it might have had but vodka has traditionally been produced in the east with a variety of flavourings, including cinnamon, ginger, various fruits and flowers, vanilla, chocolate and pepper. In Poland, leaves of bison grass are used to produce Zubrowka and vodka made with honey is called krupnik.

Some vodka mixes can actually be incredibly useful, especially for motorists. One former Polish MP, Grzegorz Gruszka, was stopped by the police during a routine check and failed a breath test but managed to wriggle out of a driving ban by proving that he had not drunk any alcohol. He had used a mixture of vodka and mustard, known as 'jogobelka', as a mouthwash, swilling it round his mouth without actually swallowing any. It is unlikely, however, that telling your local traffic cops, anywhere other than in Poland, that all you've had is a jogobelka, is going to do you any good whatsoever.

Janglies

Similar in many ways to the jitters (see below), the janglies are a result of
that peculiar phase of the hangover that leaves all of your senses working
at 175 per cent normal efficiency. You can hear someone flicking a light
switch in a bedroom three houses away and that bird chirping outside
your window sounds like it has its own PA sysem. The sun seems like it's
about to turn supernova and it's hard to accept any colour other than
grey – everything else is just too bright. Take precautions (see *Sunglasses*)
to avoid these moments of heightened sensory perception as they can
come as a complete shock to the system, causing an attack of the janglies
– heart-stopping moments of sheer terror – like standing next to the fire
alarm when it suddenly goes off. Getting seriously jangled may even
result in the need for a change of underwear.

Jitters

'The jitters' is a strange phenomenon that affects hangover sufferers,
giving you anything from shivers up your spine and momentary
trembling of the fingers to shaky knees and an uncontrollable twitching
of the eye. The jitters will make it impossible for you to perform tasks
that require any degree of skill, like threading a needle, inserting a
contact lens or putting on your socks.

Jive

You thought you could last night and everyone now has a photo on their phone of you on your arse on the dance floor to prove that you can't.

Joke

Yes, you did tell the one about the nun, the barrel and the Great Dane to your girlfriend's parents. You will probably find that she is now your ex-girlfriend.

Juice

Orange juice or any other citrus fruit juice is good for topping up your Vitamin C to fight off the hangover. If it says concentrate on the bottle, that means you can dilute it with water, not that you have to think really hard about it.

Jungle

The jungle can be a noisy place with parrots screeching, monkeys whooping and birds and insects twittering and chirping away. The good thing about jungles is that they are far away. The bad thing about hangovers is that there's a jungle going on inside your brain. This sensation may be linked in a mystic, primeval way to the fabled home of the ultimate hangover cure in the jungles of Cambodia (see *Ang-naff-nang*).

The Best Medicine

A man was digging up a flower bed in his front garden when he unearthed an old lamp. He rubbed some dirt off it and as he did so – Whoosh! – a genie appeared.

'You have freed me from the lamp,' said the genie. 'I may now grant you the customary three wishes.'

'Wow!' gasped the man. 'Well, I wish that my trouser pocket would always have a £50 note in it no matter how many times I take one out.'

Woosh!

The man put his hand in his pocket and pulled out a £50 note. Then he pulled out another, and another, and another.

'Brilliant!' he cheered. 'Now I'd like a bright red Ferrari Daytona, please!'

Woosh!

The beautiful classic Ferrari appeared next to the old Ford Focus on the man's driveway.

'Fantastic!' cried the man, stroking the car's bonnet. 'Now all I want is for you to make me irresistible to women.'

Woosh!

He turned into a box of chocolates.

Sure Cure

MINT TEA

You're probably used to your morning cuppa being piping hot. Maybe you even have to let it stand for a while to cool a bit before you take your first sip. You don't drink it out of the saucer, do you? Tea is good for hangovers because it gets some liquid back into your system to fight the dehydration caused by the alcohol. How about a cup of cold tea? Disgusting? Not at all. You can buy all sorts of iced tea in your local lunchtime sandwich takeaway these days and mint tea is one of the most refreshing. The minty aroma certainly helps to make you feel a bit more clear-headed.

> 1 large cup of cold tea (no, you don't put milk in it)
> 3 or 4 sprigs of fresh mint
> 1 teaspoon of sugar

It's best to have chilled the tea in the fridge for an hour or so before you add the mint and sugar. Then serve it in a glass with plenty of ice.

HANGOVERS IN HISTORY

Fotheringhay Castle, England, 1587

Ma mooth feels like the bottom o' a budgie's cage.

Mine too, my dear – with the budgie still in it.

It was a grand way tae celebrate ma last night in the castle.

Nice of everyone to turn up to see you off this morning, too.

Dae ye think they feel as bog awful as I do?

I doubt it. You Scots are famous drinkers.

Wooses. They'll be sorry if I puke ma guts up right in front o' them.

Not as sorry as me. I'd have to clear it up.

Ma shoulders hurt as much as ma hied.

I'm not surprised. They told you you could never lift a chair with a fully-armed pikeman sitting on it.

I think I can dae anything when I've the drink in me. I should have listened tae them.

So should I. Now I can hardly lift my arms.

Ye fairly surprised the hell oot o' the pikeman, though.

Yes, but now I'll have to pay to have the pike hole in the ceiling repaired.

I'm glad I'm no' payin' fur it.

That's another thing you Scots are famous for.

Cheeky bugger! Ye had better be fit to dae a good job for me.

I'll do my best. How's the head?

It's pure burstin', so it is – driving me mental.

Well, I've got the best cure for that.

And that's a fact, or my name's no' Mary, Queen of Scots.

That's right, my dear. Now just pop your neck on the block and I'll try to swing this damned axe . . .

Kaleidoscope Effect

When you stumble out of bed with the mother of all hangovers, don't be tempted to pick up the remote to switch on a spot of breakfast television. Staring at a TV screen while hungover can easily bring on the kaleidoscope effect with those happy, smiley breakfast-TV presenters' faces all blurring and merging and separating again just like in a kid's kaleidoscope toy. If you don't know what a kid's kaleidoscope does, on no account try looking into one with a hangover.

Kangaroo Thighs

Prolonged confinement in the bog, either sitting or kneeling, can result in a stiffening of the joints and muscle seizure that leaves you crouched over, able only to make short hopping movements with kangaroo thighs. There is also a danger that, just like on a long-haul flight (and let's face it you could be in there for a long haul), you could contract Deep Vein Thrombosis. For goodness' sake get up and walk around a bit, just don't stray too far from the crapper.

Karate

Nowadays it seems like everyone has offspring or younger relatives learning karate or some other martial art. Kids watch the Turtles kicking ass, think, 'Cowabunga! I could do that!' and sign up for classes. It might be fun to let them practise on you when you are sober, but when you are hungover, your reaction time is dulled and you are liable to cop a quick kick in the Niagaras. If one of these junior ninjas comes anywhere near you, run away and hide.

Karaoke

Yes, you did hog the mic and insist on singing 'Wonderwall' over and over again until you got it just right. This will now replay constantly in your mind throughout the morning. Find a small child who wants to practise karate (see above). Only that kind of pain can take your mind off your karaoke performances.

King Kong

The big monkey did not hold your girlfriend perfectly still with one hand then whirl you all over the dance floor with the other, bouncing you off the floor and crashing you into tables. You dreamt that. Something amazingly similar did actually happen . . . just no monkey.

Knees

If you are suffering from painful grazing on the knees, see *Friction Burns*, *Chin*, *Elbows*, *Nose* and *Forehead*.

Strange But True . . .

During the Second World War, rationing and the priority given in industry to essential production for the war effort meant that many things became short in supply. Whisky, along with other spirits, was one of the items that became difficult to get hold of, so certain enterprising individuals set out to make their own – to be sold at a huge profit on the black market, of course.

Unfortunately, their methods of production were not quite as exacting as those of the mainstream whisky distillers. The stuff the black marketeers produced was called 'hooch' and some of the concoctions they came up with were just thinly disguised industrial alcohol. A little food colouring and maybe some flavouring added to each bottle gave it a passing resemblance to whisky. Hooch wasn't for back-room parties – it was sold to hotels and nightclubs. RAF crews were warned that even a small tipple of the spirits on sale in some London clubs might cause temporary blindness. Getting drunk on it could leave you permanently blinded, insane or dead. American servicemen going out on the town were sometimes given bottles of American whiskey before leaving their barracks to stop them buying the counterfeit Scotch. A storm in a teacup (or whisky tumbler)? Not at all. More than a dozen people died in Glasgow in May 1942 from drinking hooch and four businessmen who popped into a hotel in London for a quick 'whisky' were left paralysed for ten days!

When I was seventeen
I drank some very good beer
I drank some very good beer
I purchased with a fake ID
My name was Brian McGee
I stayed up listening to Queen
When I was seventeen

HOMER SIMPSON

The Best Medicine

A man walks into a bar with Michael Schumacher's head poking out of his flies. The man nods to the barman, Schumacher nods to the barman, and then the man orders a beer. The barman carefully pours the beer and passes it across the bar.

'Excuse me for asking,' said the barman, 'but isn't that Michael Schumacher down the front of your trousers?'

'Yeah,' sighs the man. 'He's driving me nuts.'

Sure Cure

TREAD GINGERLY

You don't actually have to tread the fruit for this drink – that would be asking a bit too much in your condition – and attempting to tread apples and carrots would just leave you with a load of mulch between your toes, anyway. What you really need for this is a juicer. If you don't have a juicer, forget it. Any other method is going to be far too complicated for anyone with a hangover to cope with. A bit like Cold Carrot (see page 45), the noise that the juicer makes might be enough to put you off, but the end result is worth it.

> 4 apples
> 4 carrots
> Sprinkling of ground ginger

Use more apples or carrots depending on how much juice you want to make. The beauty of a juicer machine is that it separates the skins and cores and provides you with just the juice. Put the apples and carrots (give them a good scrub first) in the juicer and sprinkle the ginger onto the mix that comes out. Give it a stir and serve with ice.

Laughter

Often called the best medicine but do not attempt it with a hangover. Your entire skull is made of the finest crystal and could crack very easily.

Lavatory

Rehearse and remember the way to the nearest one before you go to bed to avoid making the morning hangover an even worse experience (see *Lost*).

Legs

Take great care when you first get out of bed as your legs may set off in almost any direction and often several directions at once. You will soon regain control but you will feel a general weakness in the lower limbs, caused mainly by walking five miles in the wrong direction last night trying to find a taxi willing to take you home. This weakness is exacerbated by the effects of your foolhardiness in the curry house (see *Chicken Ringstinger*).

Lie

This is what you must do when you phone in to work having woken up half an hour after you were supposed to be there. Tell them anything. A death in the family always works well, as long as it's not your own.

Lie-In

When you wake up with a hangover the best thing to do is go straight back to sleep. This comes perfectly naturally to some people, but others may need to practise.

Liver

You really should be kinder to your liver. It is the second largest organ in your body, the largest being your skin. The liver is a kind of chemical plant sitting just below your chest. It produces all sorts of stuff that your body needs but is almost as useless as you are when it becomes overloaded with alcohol. Be nice to your liver and drink nothing but water for a couple of days to give it a rest. It will reward you by keeping you alive for a while longer.

Lost

As the fog of your hangover slowly starts to lift, you will realize that you lost many things last night (see *Missing*), including your head, your temper and control of your bowels. You may even have got lost yourself, not only on the way home but simply on the way to the bathroom. Turn left instead of right and you open the door to a closet or, worse, your parents' bedroom. You will immediately be able to tell by the look on your mum's face if you staggered into her room in the middle of the night and pissed on the dressing table . . . again.

HANGOVERS IN HISTORY

Atlantic Ocean, near Portugal, 1872

Open the door! What the hell are you doing in there?

Same as most people do in a toilet.

You've been in there for ages.

I feel safe in here.

I'm not surprised! You've stunk out everywhere else. There's a brown mist hanging in the air.

It was those spicy bagels and dried chillies we got in New York.

Nothing to do with the alcohol you've been pilfering for days, then?

It's powerful stuff.

It's industrial alcohol, you're not supposed to drink it.

Packs a helluva punch when you do drink it.

Packs a helluva punch when it blasts your guts out the other end, too.

You're not making me feel better.

You don't deserve to feel better. That stuff will make you go blind. In the meantime, the stench is choking everyone else around here!

That's why I feel safe in here.

You're joking! You mean you've locked yourself in the only place that you haven't contaminated?

Not so far but . . . OH!! There goes another one! Stand back! I'm coming out!

No chance. Stay in there and suffer like the rest of us.

Gaaaaaaaaah . . . it's eating all the air . . . let go of the door . . .

Only if you promise to stick a cork in it.

Help me, I'm dying . . .

Okay, come out, then, but it's hardly any better out here.

Let's get out on deck before we suffocate.

Hey, where the hell is everyone?

Yeah, I've never known the Marie Celeste *to be so quiet.*

They've all made off in the lifeboat! Well I'm not staying here in a ghost ship full of your farts. Grab that lumber and we'll make a raft . . .

Blame It All On The Booze

GIN

Nowadays, gin enjoys the status of a rather genteel tipple – a civilized drink to be enjoyed with tonic water in drawing rooms and gentlemen's clubs. But gin was once responsible for the kind of drunken debauchery that makes your average Saturday night out look like a Bible class in Mother Theresa's back room. In eighteenth-century London, gin was so cheap and plentiful that the poorest among the population consumed it in huge quantities to render themselves immune to the squalor of their surroundings. Distilleries in the capital churned out around 10 million gallons of gin annually and the average Londoner drank about 14 gallons a year. Gin was cheaper than beer or any other kind of alcohol and so many women took to the stuff that it became known as 'mother's ruin'. The government was ultimately forced to introduce legislation covering the production and sale of gin as well as increased taxation on the spirit to try to alleviate the problem of widespread drunkenness in the capital.

Yet gin was actually first developed as a medicine intended as a cure for indigestion and kidney disorders. Franz de la Boé was Professor of Medicin at Leyden in Holland in 1650 and experimented with distilled spirits mixed with juniper oil, calling his concoction *genever*, from the French word for 'juniper', *genièvre*. When English soldiers in Holland came across this marvellous medicine, they tended to prescribe themselves rather more than could ever possibly have been good for their health, spreading the word – albeit the shortened word 'gin' – when they got back home. The soldiers found that they fought far more bravely when they had taken some of this miracle medicine, hence the term 'Dutch courage'. Mind you, anyone swaying around with a bucketful of gin inside them is going to make a pretty difficult target.

As well as being at least partially responsible for the widespread abuse of gin, the military can also claim to have had a hand in its gentrification through the gin and tonic. In far-flung corners of Britain's Empire in the east, malaria was endemic, claiming the lives of countless soldiers and administrators. It was discovered that quinine, an ingredient in tonic water, could help to fight the disease. Since plain tonic water went down about as well as a cup of cold sick, good old gin was added, along with a slice of lime and a couple of ice cubes to tart it up – and the 'G & T' was invented.

In America, gin vied with whisky as the most popular spirit before vodka came along, and the Americans can lay claim to having invented gin martinis, a favourite in the speakeasy bars during the prohibition years. Drinking straight gin is not an easy skill to master, so it is most popular with mixers, although a 'pink gin' is almost neat. In a pink gin, a drop of angostura bitters (an extract of gentian and spices) is swilled around the glass before the gin is added. This was a tipple championed by the Royal Navy, many officers believing that the angostura bitters helped prevent seasickness. The other theory is that, after a few pink gins, you wouldn't give a monkey's about feeling sick.

Martial Arts

The shooting pain down the back of your leg is there to confirm that you cannot perform flying backward kicks like Bruce Lee, however much you may have thought you could at the bus stop last night.

Missing

Weren't you wearing a jacket when you went out last night? Didn't you have a lot more money in your trouser pocket? Didn't you have trousers on? How can all these things have gone missing? If you're not sure of the answer – phone a friend. They are usually only too happy to remind you just what you got up to.

Money

Don't even bother checking your pockets. You spent it all.

Morning After

The only good thing about experiencing the morning after the night before is that it proves you didn't die in your sleep. At the time you may wonder whether that was a good thing or not . . .

Morning Glory

If you wake up lying on your back and there's a mound in the duvet that makes it look like you went to sleep in a tent, you are undoubtedly experiencing the Morning Glory, a certain part of your anatomy having risen rather earlier than you did. Calm yourself, stud, as this is more likely to be due to a bladder that's full-to-bursting creating pressure that has hoisted the mainsail than it is to your overwhelming sex drive. Your next question is, 'Should I attempt to have sex, on a hangover, even if I am flying solo?' Oh, for goodness' sake go take a leak.

Motion Sickness

So you weren't feeling as bad as you thought you should when you first woke up. You even managed a slice of toast before leaving for work. But as soon as you got on the bus or the train and it started to move, motion sickness kicked in. The only way to deal with this is to get off again at the next stop. The last thing you want to do is to barf on the bus or chunder on the train. You may not know all those people very well, but you'll have to face them again every morning on the way to work – and however anonymous you might feel on your regular commute, no one is going to forget the filthy swine who threw up on their Hush Puppies. Get off and go home.

The Best Medicine

Two old friends who had been out drinking the night before met up at a local cafe for breakfast, severely hungover.

'Why have you got a suppository stuck in your ear?' said the first bloke.

'Eh?' said his friend.

'I said,' said the first man, a bit louder, 'why have you got a suppository stuck in your ear?'

His friend plucked the thing out of his ear and stared at it for a second.

'Thanks,' he said. 'Now I know where I put my hearing aid.'

Sure Cure

GROGGY NOGGY

An eggnog is not just for Christmas. It's not even just for winter. It is, however, a great settler of the stomach and general hangover healer. Everyone knows that eggs are good for you and so is milk; eggs provide essential amino acids and milk gives us calcium that many believe helps to calm the nerves – just what you need if you're suffering from the jitters or the janglies (see page 74). Brandy and rum might not seem to be quite as healthy but, let's face it, you didn't get your hangover by being a dedicated health freak anyway.

> 1 measure brandy
> 1 measure rum
> 1 egg
> 1 large spoonful of cocktail syrup
> 3 measures milk
> Sprinkling of ground nutmeg

Put the brandy, rum, egg and syrup into a cocktail shaker and do your best to give it a vigorous shake. Have a little sit down if you need it, then pour the mix into a large glass. Stir gently (the drink that is, not you, unless you've nodded off again) as you add the milk, then sprinkle the nutmeg on top.

A TO Z OF HANGOVERS N

Nadgers
See *Genitals*.

Neanderthal
When you're walking to work hunched over and dragging your knuckles along the pavement like some kind of evolutionary throw-back, cheer yourself up with the thought that the Neanderthal's brain was actually bigger than yours is. Clearly, he didn't feel he needed such a big brain in order to evolve into a moron like you.

Neck
The nasty bruise on the back of your neck that feels like you were kung-fued by Bruce Lee was more likely caused when the toilet seat kept falling on your head.

Negligence
A strange early morning hangover condition that affects wives and girlfriends who bumble downstairs in their skimpiest nighty, completely forgetting that you left three mates sleeping on the living-room floor.

Niagaras
See *Nadgers*.

Nipples

An interesting symptom of the hangover is having mysteriously bruised nipples, even displaying the odd bite mark here and there. Suffice to say that you didn't do this to yourself unless you fell downstairs and landed on your false teeth . . . over and over again. So just who the hell were you getting down and dirty with last night?

Nose

If your nose looks like you tried to reshape it with sandpaper last night, there are a number of explanations for this phenomenon. Showing off on the way home by attempting to dive from a six-foot wall into a polystyrene carton of tomato soup could be one of them, but see also *Elbows*, *Forehead*, *Chin* and *Friction Burns*.

Nudity

A typical feature of the morning-after hangover is to wake up naked. You may wonder where all your clothes went. Your friends will shortly be texting and phoning to tell you all about it.

Nux Vomica

A homeopathic remedy that can be helpful for trapped wind, bloating and an upset stomach, and some have suggested it as a hangover cure. Given that it contains strychnine and can be immensely poisonous, you'd better be pretty careful with it. You will recover from your hangover by tomorrow, but there's no bouncing back from the mortuary slab.

I'd hate to be a teetotaller.
Imagine waking up
in the morning
and knowing that's
as good
as you're going to
feel all day.

W. C. FIELDS

Strange But True . . .

People living in the town of Tweed Heads, on the Tweed River in New South Wales, Australia, might have renamed their river 'Beer Creek' when they discovered that, if they fancied a bottle or two, all they had to do was jump in the water. Scattered on the river bed were 24,000 bottles of beer, the result of an accident when the trailer of a truck lost a wheel and careered down the river bank.

Scores of locals were soon on the scene, diving into the river to collect bottles, some even using scuba gear to reach the sunken treasure, before loading up their cars. Naughty – everyone knows you shouldn't take a drink and then drive. One particularly thirsty beer hunter reportedly made off with around 400 bottles, although the local police eventually advised everyone that this was not a free-for-all and that what they were doing was simple theft. There is no truth in the rumour that the police car then drove off with the sound of clinking bottles coming from its boot.

HANGOVERS IN HISTORY

Southampton, England, 1912

I don't believe you let us sleep for half the bloody day.

Shut up and keep running.

Run? I can barely walk. My legs are like rubber.

They served you well enough last night dancing with that floosie . . .

Ah, she was a cracker, wasn't she?

. . . and her sister . . . and her mother . . .

She was a great kisser.

Which one? You had a go at all three.

Only two of them slapped me, though.

Yeah, but the mother kneed you in the goolies. Did dipping them in that jug of bee actually help any?

It helped get us thrown out of the pub. Damn! Now I've got a nail sticking through the sole of my boot.

You should have taken them to the menders.

Cobblers.

It was only a suggestion.

Slow down – last night's fish and chips feels like it's about to reappear.

I know what you mean. It's only that pickled egg you made me swallow whole that's keeping mine down.

I didn't make you do it. It was a bet.

Yeah, like you bet I'd never get us these jobs and I did.

Well, now I bet you I'll drop dead if we don't stop running.

All right, we'll walk, but keep it brisk.

Brisk it is, just let me relight my fag. It blew out we were running so fast.

How can you smoke and run at the same time?

If I knew that I wouldn't have to relight my fag.

I won't be able to face another cigarette for days, I feel so bad.

I can't live without smoke. I'm used to working in the boiler room.

Well you won't be working in a boiler room for a while – look! She's pulling out!

We've missed it! We'll lose all our pay! My wife will kill me!

And mine! And we'll certainly never be offered jobs on the Titanic *again . . .*

Oasis

Just in case you'd forgotten – 'Wonderwall'. (See *Karaoke*.)

Occult

The hangover demons cannot be banished by draping garlic round your neck and sleeping in a pentangle drawn on the floor while holding a cross made from two wooden spoons sellotaped together. Your mate with the digital camera just wants a picture for his blog.

'Oh God . . .'

It is something of a miracle how many people find religion while sitting or kneeling in the smallest room in the house. Just like Saul en route to Damascus, your enlightenment may come en route to the tabernacle of the bathroom. Pray first that it's not occupied.

'Oh Noooo . . .'

This will be your mantra as, piece by piece, the things you did and the things you said come creeping back through the hangover memory mist.

Oops!

Blundering around in a hungover haze, you will find that you become incredibly clumsy. Coffee will be spilled, milk bottles become unmanageable, things fall over and smash on the floor when you have hardly even touched them. Don't blame yourself. It's not your fault. There is a poltergeist in your house following you around, feeding off the misery of your hangover. It will be banished from the premises once you shake off your hangover . . . until the next time.

Oranges

They are packed with Vitamin C but are highly dangerous. You should not attempt to use a knife to cut one – not in your condition. Sticking your thumb into the skin is equally hazardous as a jet of pure orange juice can squirt straight in your eye and set your hangover recovery back by half an hour. Get someone else to peel one for you.

Oxygen

If you are lucky enough to work in a hospital or medical practice you may be able to sneak a whiff of oxygen now and again. Medics swear by this as a hangover remedy. Don't take the helium by mistake. Wandering around bleary-eyed talking like Mickey Mouse is a dead giveaway that you've been up to something.

Blame It All On The Booze

RUM

Allegedly, Winston Churchill once said, 'Don't talk to me about naval tradition. It's nothing but rum, sodomy and the lash.' I suppose that could explain why so many sailors who have drunk themselves senseless on rum aboard ship wake up with a helluva sore arse. Rum is, nevertheless, closely associated with the Royal Navy, sailors having enjoyed a daily ration of rum since around 1655 when the British captured Jamaica. Prior to having a rum ration, the sailors were given French brandy, sodomy and the lash. To avoid having his crews rolling around drunk on deck, Admiral Edward Vernon decreed that the rum should be watered down before it was issued and the mixture became known as grog, named after the grogram (a fabric of silk and wool waterproofed with gum) cloak worn by the admiral in foul weather. A rum ration was still given to British sailors up to July 1970.

One story has it that when Admiral Nelson was killed at the Battle of Trafalgar in 1805 his body was preserved in a barrel of rum for its return to England. When the barrel was opened, however, there was no rum left, the sailors having drilled a hole in the barrel so that they could drink the rum – and Nelson's blood along with it. This is said by some to be the origin of the naval toast 'Nelson's Blood'. Yuck.

With the Caribbean in the hands of the British, the French and the British and French pirates, Americans began to fret about how to get their hands on enough rum to keep the colonists happy, so the first American rum distillery was built on Staten Island in 1664. It soon became one of the new world's most profitable industries, with each member of the American population drinking roughly 3 gallons of rum every year. George Washington had a barrel of rum at his inauguration as President in 1789, although he didn't drink it all himself.

The rum ration originally enjoyed by those seventeenth-century seamen would have been a sweet, dark concoction distilled from molasses which was produced during the process of refining sugar from sugar cane. The fact that the molasses would ferment into alcohol was probably discovered by the slaves working on the sugar-cane plantations but it certainly would not have taken long for the plantation bosses to realize that the slaves were on to a good thing. Distilling the fermented molasses was a way of purifying it and increasing its potency. The first rum produced in the Caribbean was almost certainly rough, powerful stuff but once the distillation process used became more sophisticated, so too did the end product. Rums that were light in colour, or completely clear, sat alongside the darker brews, and rum grew to become one of the most versatile spirits of all. It is used to make punch, flavoured with spices, widely used in cocktails and drunk with all manner of mixers. It is used as a flavouring in all sorts of dishes, especially in cakes, and as the base for a number of liqueurs.

Rum, sodomy and the lash? Given the choice, I'd like the rum, please, Winston.

The Best Medicine

Drinking and sex don't always mix, so here are the top ten reasons why a beer and a shag are so different.

1. You can always get a beer.

2. You can have too much head with your beer.

3. You get no hassle from a beer you just dropped.

4. You would puke if you got a hair in your teeth while having a beer.

5. You can enjoy a beer if it's a bit yeasty.

6. You can have a beer with someone of the same sex and nobody will care.

7. You can have a beer in front of your auntie.

8. You can wear a condom and still enjoy your beer.

9. You pay tax for every beer you drink.

10. You have a problem if you like a beer first thing in the morning.

Sure Cure

FRUIT FEST

Get some Vitamin C inside you with the Fruit Fest. Unlike so many other hangover cures, this one is entirely healthy, so not only can you feel it doing you good, you can enjoy that self-righteous feeling along with it. This will encourage you to straighten your back and stand tall, proud that you've consumed something healthy for a change. Resist the temptation to add a slug of vodka to give it a kick as that will leave you all curled up, shrivelled and moany like you were when you woke up.

> 2 oranges
> 2 kiwi fruits
> 4 large strawberries
> Squeeze of lemon juice
> 1 slice of bread

Put the fruit in the blender, having peeled and chopped the oranges and the kiwi fruit and de-stalked the strawberries. Tear the slice of bread in half, squash one slice in each hand until it goes doughy and then stick it in your ears so that you don't have to suffer the noise when you switch on the blender. Pour the blended fruit mix into a glass with lots of ice. Remember to take the bread out of your ears before you set off for work.

Pain

It's in your head, back, joints and stomach; it's become your constant companion. As we all know, the Devil invented hangovers and the pain is caused by him attempting to rip out your soul. Drink a cup of coffee, take a couple of Neurofen and stop being such a wuss.

Palpitations

Too much fizzy lager late at night and a Chinese takeaway laced with MSGs can easily have you waking up in the middle of the night with the feeling that the entire cast of *Watership Down* is mating on your chest. Have a glass of water, take a few easy breaths and calm down. You will know if it's a heart attack because you'll wake up dead.

Parp

When you're sitting there with the bloated feeling that you think can only be eased by lifting a cheek and releasing a sneaky (and secret) guff, think again. Your bottom has a mind all of its own during a hangover and will blast out a fanfare that will make the Band of the Grenadier Guards sound like a mouse playing a penny whistle. Don't risk it.

Peak

You will peak and trough throughout your hangover. Peaks come when you feel momentary relief, a brief euphoria, perhaps as a result of an energy release in the form of a sugar rush from that chocolate doughnut you just ate. Savour the moment; it won't last. (See *Trough*.)

Penis Dysfunction

You might be the randiest little terrier in town but with a full-blown hangover your senses will be so dulled and the nauseous feeling so intense that a Brazilian carnival samba dancer and a nymphomaniac Swedish Olympic high-jumper will fail to raise even a smile. Give in and admit that, for this morning at least, you are home to Mr Floppy.

Pish

As in 'Thish beer'sh pish.' Derived from 'piss', the vernacular term for urine. In Northern Ireland it's pronounced 'posh' but that still doesn't make it a compliment.

Poltergeist

See *Occult*.

Puke

Far from being just another word for 'vomit', 'puke' is a highly descriptive, onomatopoeic noun best used with reference to an involuntary or otherwise unwanted vomit. The 'p' at beginning implies a reluctant pursing of the lips and the 'pop' of them being forced open. The 'u' sound gives us the traumatic and despairing 'oooooooh' of pain and the 'ke' is quite simply a truncated 'KERRRIIIST ALMIGHTY!!!'

*The problem with the world
is that everyone is a
few drinks behind.*

HUMPHREY BOGART

Part 3
Barf To The Future

Once you've actually made it to the kitchen (see page 61), what's your next move? You desperately need to get some liquid inside you. Make sure you drink plenty of water to replace lost fluid and fruit juice for the vitamins. Go on, have a cup of coffee, but remember that you will need to drink even more water to combat the fact that the coffee will make you need to pee. So what else will make you feel better? Sadly, there is no instant cure, but burn yourself some toast to get started. The carbon in the burned bread will soak up some of the toxins in your system and at least help to stop you feeling any worse. In hospitals, they pump a carbon mixture into the stomachs of people with alcohol poisoning to stop the toxins from killing them.

You've got to eat something. Bananas are good. They replace the potassium you pissed away last night, they'll give you some energy and they are easy to eat – mash them up on your burned toast. Try a sports drink or two as well. They help to replace lost sugar and minerals. Take a look at some of the Sure Cures scattered throughout this book, too. Many of them are known to help certain people feel remarkably better. You need to experiment to see which ones work for you.

Some people will now tell you that what you need is a huge fried breakfast. Others will feel a chunder brewing at the mere thought. Eating fatty food can easily have the effect of irritating an already delicate stomach and the whole lot could quickly reappear at ten times the speed you wolfed it down. The same can be true of painkillers. Take great care when using them as a hangover cure because you already have lots of chemical imbalances in your system and if you are prone to a dicky tummy, they can make you feel worse.

Only you can tell what you need to eat to combat your hangover. Trial and error is the only way to find out, although it may not be pleasant to be in the same room with you when you're experiencing an error. Eating healthy food a little at a time throughout the morning to give you some energy and nutrition is probably the best advice. That fried breakfast, though, should not be dismissed entirely as it can have beneficial effects – just maybe not at breakfast time. The time to eat fatty foods is actually before you start drinking. They stick to the lining of your stomach and slow the rate at which alcohol is absorbed into your bloodstream. This means it will take you longer to get legless, but it will also give your body more time to deal with the toxins and consequently reduce the severity of your hangover.

The idea of taking something to prevent a hangover before you start drinking is not a new one. Eating a hearty meal to 'line your stomach' before a drinking session is one way of doing it but different cultures have had different solutions to the problem for centuries. In some Mediterranean countries a swig of olive oil was recommended to give the same effect as a fry-up. A couple of teaspoons of evening primrose oil is a similar suggestion, as is eating peanut butter. A teaspoon of Bifidus powder in a glass of water before going to bed is believed to combat the effects of acetaldehyde and some American Indians would eat a handful of raw almonds to help them drink without getting drunk. Drink without getting drunk? What kind of crazy talk is that?

University Research in California has shown that taking an extract of the prickly pear cactus five hours before drinking will help reduce hangover symptoms, but that's just about as daft as the Indians and their nuts. Who on earth is going to know five hours beforehand that they'll end up lagered and then have the common sense to be carrying a prickly pear cactus with them just in case?

One supposed hangover cure that is not for the faint-hearted is to have sex. Some say that getting the blood pumping round your body, raising your metabolic rate with the exercise and sending adrenalin coursing through your system will wipe out your hangover in no time. And you might even enjoy yourself. Human beings and dolphins are the only animals that have sex purely for pleasure. You can never find a dolphin when you want one, though, can you? And should you have sex before you start drinking, after you've been drinking (in which case the argument just may not stand up), or when you wake up with the full-blown hangover? Or all three? Or maybe even while you're having a drink? Where on earth are you going to find the time to get down to the pub?

Perhaps one answer to the hangover conundrum is to take a close look not only at what you drink, but also how much and how often. Of course, if you drink enough often enough you may never actually sober up enough to suffer from a hangover in the first place. Do you find yourself spending more and more time arguing with the washing machine or talking to your invisible friend at the bus stop? Do mosquitoes fall to the ground after biting you and then stagger about singing 'Come On Eileen'?

Ultimately, of course, the only way to avoid a hangover is to stop drinking alcohol. If you do this you will undoubtedly live much longer. That, however, will only prolong the torture, giving you all those extra years to remember the taste of the last beer you ever had. You don't want to be that sad teetotaller with his nose pressed against the pub window, so rule that out straightaway and move on to the next most radical solution – kidney dialysis. Unfortunately, not everyone has easy access to a dialysis machine and a medical team, but if you did, the pretty nurses (they're all pretty when you've had a skinful) can have you hooked up to the machine in minutes. A mere five hours later the machine will have filtered your blood far more efficiently than your kidneys could manage in your state.

Is that it then? Stop drinking, go on dialysis, carry a cactus around or eat an Indian's nuts? Is there no other way of avoiding the dreaded hangover? There are folk remedies galore and countless products available over the counter at your local pharmacist. The truth is that only you can figure out exactly what combination of preventative measures and morning after palliatives will work for you. You simply have to go out, get drunk, and try them all out until you find that magic silver bullet.

Good luck!

The Best Medicine

A monstrously large woman wearing a white vest and jeans slouched into a pub, lifted one arm above her head to reveal a massively hairy armpit and called, 'Is there a man here who will buy this lady a drink?' Some way down the bar, a drunk, squinting through glasses almost as thick as his pint pot, pulled a £5 note out of his pocket and said to the barman, 'This is to buy a drink for the ballerina.'

The women ordered a pint of Guinness, downed it in one and wiped her mouth on the back of her hand. Then she raised her other arm in the air, showing another jungle of hair in her armpit and asked, 'Is there any other man who will buy this lady a drink?'

The same short-sighted drunk offered his money to the bartender.

'This is to buy the ballerina a drink,' he said.

'Do you know this lady, sir?' asked the barman.

'Not at all,' replied the drunk.

'Then why do you keep calling her "the ballerina"?' the barman asked.

'Surely it's obvious?' said the drunk. 'Any lady who can lift her leg that far in the air has got to be a ballerina!'

Sure Cure

THE SMOOTHIE

No, it's not a description of the sophisticated, witty, debonair young man-about-town that you thought you were last night. 'Burbling plonker' might be nearer the mark for that. Smoothies are great, non-alcoholic refreshers, ideal for anyone too hungover to face a proper breakfast or a proper hair of the dog in any form. You can use all sorts of fruit to make smoothies, and you needn't even use natural yoghurt – a good flavoured yoghurt, especially if it already has chunks of fruit in it, will do just as well. Try experimenting with a few different combinations – such as pear and mango, apple and plum or papaya and passion fruit – some other time when you're feeling up to it.

> 1 large banana
> 1 mango
> 300 ml milk
> 150 ml yoghurt

Peel the banana and the mango, also removing the stone from the mango. Place the banana, mango, milk and yoghurt in a blender and whizz until it's completely smooth. Serve in a glass with ice.

Quaffing

Having been quaffing beer, wine, or whatever your chosen poison is, all
night long, you now need to quaff plenty of water or fruit juice to ease
the passage of the dreaded hangover. Hypotonic or isotonic sports drinks
contain much-needed minerals and it is believed that they are absorbed
into your system far faster than plain water. Quaffing gallons of coffee
may ease a headache but it will make you pee more and you then lose
even more essential fluid.

Queasy

That unsettled queasy feeling is going to plague you until you get
something inside you to help calm your stomach. Something simple like
toast or pasta will do the job, especially if you drink something soothing
like chamomile tea at the same time. Chicken soup will probably work,
too. One ancient Middle Eastern cure involved eating a paste of myrrh
and ground-up swallow's beak. You're not likely to have a jar of that
handy to spread on your toast, though.

Queen

If, by any chance, you are due to attend a royal garden party or receive
an MBE, keep your celebrations until *after* the event. Turning up at
Buckingham Palace looking like a sack of shit and smelling like a
brewery is not the done thing, unless you are Prince Andrew. If you are

feeling a bit hungover on the day, the Queen will be hugely sympathetic. She likes the odd bevvy and has undoubtedly had a few stinkers herself.

Quiet

As a hangover precaution, write the word 'QUIET' on a piece of paper and stick it to your bedroom door before you go out drinking – you'll be in no condition to do it when you get home. That way it will be there in the morning, doing its best to persuade anyone passing your door to do so on tiptoe.

Quiff

Hangover mornings are always mad-hair days. That cute quiff you had at the front of your hair will be joined by several more at the back and sides. No amount of combing or brushing will persuade them to lie down and they have been known to survive up to half an hour under a power shower. Wear a hat.

Quit

Hangover days are the best days ever to quit smoking, quit drinking and quit eating too much. Quitting eating altogether is not a good idea, but having a hangover is good for dieting – especially the headache. Banging your head against a wall apparently uses up to 150 calories an hour.

*I work until
beer o'clock.*

STEPHEN KING

Strange But True . . .

In the early part of the nineteenth century, English society boozer Squire Jack Mytton used to drink around six bottles of port every day. He was also addicted to gambling and would do anything for a bet, even going hunting in the nude. He also once made a grand entrance riding a bear into the dining room. Inevitably, he ended up with huge debts and fled the country. He carried on drinking, though, and in Calais in 1830 he tried to cure an attack of the hiccups by setting his shirt on fire. He died in a debtors' prison in London two years later aged just thirty-seven.

Blame It All On The Booze

BRANDY

Like all forms of alcohol, brandy can be very confusing, especially if you've had a few. There are so many different names to try to get your head round and so many different kinds of brandy. Needless to say, all of them will easily supply you with the hangover from hell, and it doesn't really help at that stage to understand what it was that made you so drunk, so try to soak all this up now while you're still sober – you are sober, aren't you?

You can divide brandy into three different main types – pomace brandy, fruit brandy and grape brandy.

Pomace brandy is distilled from fermented grape pulp, seeds and stems – the stuff that is left after the juice has been squeezed out to make wine. The Italian *grappa* and French *marc* are both pomace brandies.

Fruit brandy is distilled from fruits other than grapes and is made using apples, raspberries, peaches, plums, apricots or almost any other soft fruit you can think of. Calvados is apple brandy, *kirschwasser* is made from cherries and *slivovitz* comes from plums.

Grape brandy is what most people are talking about when they ask for a brandy and it has a long and illustrious history. It was probably first produced many centuries ago by boiling wine in a cauldron covered with a sheepskin. The sheepskin would absorb the alcohol as it evaporated and could then be wrung out to extract the alcohol. Thankfully, the distillation process has come on a bit since then. Such early techniques were also probably only used on the less palatable wines, basically making use of the stuff that nobody wanted to drink.

There are a few different kinds of grape brandy. American brandy is produced in California, where there is a thriving wine industry, and brandy is also produced in South Africa, Spain and just about everywhere else that produces wine. Cognac is brandy from the Cognac region of France and Armagnac is from the Armagnac region further south.

Brandies of different quality are aged in wooden casks and labelled using a lettering system – V.S., is Very Special and around three years old; V.S.O.P. is Very Superior Old Pale, aged for five years; and X.O. is Extra Old, having been aged for over six years. One of the most famous cognac producers, Hennessy, was started by Richard Hennessy, an Irish mercenary who fought for the King of France and was rewarded with a parcel of land near the town of Cognac in 1765. The company was the first to use a 'star' system to label its cognac – basically the more stars you see, the better the cognac.

Brandy is traditionally enjoyed as an after-dinner drink but in the Cognac region they drink it all the time – after dinner, before dinner, during dinner – they probably draw the line at breakfast. Basically, they produce so much of the stuff that they need everyone to drink a lot more and are keen to promote it as a refreshing drink with, for example, tonic and ice. Give it a go – you know you've drunk worse.

Raw

The best word to describe your throat after a retch (see *Retch*), your sphincter after a curry, your bloodshot eyes, your knees after falling off the bus and the burger you bought from the van across the road from the pub.

Raw Cabbage

Some say that eating it helps cure a headache, if you can stand the damned chomping noise.

Rest

Get plenty.

Retch

A retch is just another way of describing being sick. It is just as unpleasant as all of the other ways but has some strange side-effects and involves a lot of effort for very little result. The dry retch is the worst. Your stomach pulls itself so far in that you get a hump that Quasimodo would be proud of, from somewhere just behind your tonsils you hear a kind of 'RACKATAKAKAR' noise, and tears that feel like air-gun pellets pop out from the corners of your eyes. The side effects include swollen ears from when half the blood in your body rushed into your head and a toilet seat that's been ripped in two because you were gripping it so tightly. Yet all that appears is a tiny speck of sparrow spit.

Rhino Rumba

The dance that you do when you are trying to get to the toilet in a hurry in the middle of the night. You take more footsteps than all of the contestants in a ballroom-dancing contest put together but with all the elegance and grace of a rhinoceros.

Ridiculous

It's how you behaved, it's how you look, it's how you feel, but your tongue's far too thick to let you actually say it (see *Tongue*).

Road Signs

Hungover drunks see these in their living rooms. They are not a hallucination. You stole them from the roadworks in the high street. A dead bus now lies at the bottom of a big hole as a consequence.

Rotating

Bet you never thought you'd see your eyeballs do that.

The Best Medicine

A drunk bumbles into a pub along with his pet giraffe, which is equally drunk. The man orders a beer and a gin and tonic for the giraffe. They chat and laugh until closing time when the man gets up to go but the giraffe falls asleep on the floor.

'Hey you!' yells the barman as the man makes for the door. 'You can't leave that lyin' here!'

'It's not a lion, it's a giraffe!' says the drunk.

Sure Cure

SLUSH PUPPY

Like the cold, wet nose of a puppy up the front of your dressing gown, the Slush Puppy is a real eye-opener. You'll be chilled by the ice, refreshed by the lemonade and comforted by the fact that there's a healthy glug of booze in there, too. It's definitely not recommended for one of those mornings when you have to go to work or do anything that involves any degree of concentration, joined-up writing . . . or joined-up thinking for that matter. It *is* great for a morning spent sitting in the sun contemplating going out for a lunchtime drink. Just don't let it lick you.

> 2 measures vodka
> 1 measure pineapple juice
> 1 measure lemonade
> Lots of ice

All you have to do is stick the whole lot in a blender and switch it on. Serve it in a large glass. You can vary the recipe by substituting gin for the vodka or using tomato juice instead of pineapple juice – go on, be creative.

HANGOVERS IN HISTORY

Kahuku Point, Oahu, 1941

Are you awake?

   No.

I'll take that as a 'yes.'

   How'd you like to take it as a finger in the eye?

I thought I heard something.

   That was me taking a leak.

I didn't notice you get up.

   Well, I . . . I thought I got up . . . oh, crap.

You'll soon dry off. The sun's up.

   Tell him to go back to bed.

Beautiful dawn.

   Is she here, too? Hey! Who put this sand in my bed?

You're not in bed. You're on the beach.

   How come I'm not in bed?

Because of the cops.

There're cops in my bed?

No. The cops wouldn't let us drive back to base.

We were that drunk, huh?

Yup. They stopped us and made us walk the white line on the road.

I hate white lines.

Me too. You told the cops you'd only do it if they held it still. Guess I must have tripped over an ant.

And I hate ants. I can see them crawling inside my eyelids.

Me too. And my eyes are open. Shit! There's ants crawling on the sky!

Those aren't ants – they're planes. They're coming this way.

I didn't know we had that many planes on the island.

We don't. You know, I think they're Japanese.

Now why would they be heading for Pearl Harbor at this time in the morning . . . ?

A TO Z OF HANGOVERS S

Satan

He invented the hangover and all its related ailments after being tricked by God into believing that he could suck your soul out through your toilet, starting with everything you've had to eat in the last three days. If you've ever tried to siphon fuel out of a petrol tank, you've probably got a good idea of how messy and unpleasant this is for Old Nick. He is constantly infuriated by the fact that, despite his best efforts, people end up calling down the bog to God anyway.

Scalp Stimulation

Tugging gently at your hair supposedly brings blood to your scalp and helps to relieve your headache. Obviously this is no good for slapheads.

Shakes

See *Delirium Tremens*.

Silymarin

This stuff is also called milk thistle and helps to protect your liver by acting as a barrier against toxins. You have to take it before you start drinking, preferably with a meal. That's the problem with it, really. When someone suggests popping out for a couple of drinks after work, you're going to look like a real wimp if your answer is, 'No thanks. I didn't bring my milk thistle with me.'

Sleep

If you wake up with a hangover, you haven't had enough sleep. Go back to sleep immediately unless you have woken up somewhere inappropriate, such as next to your best friend's wife, or on a railway line.

Smell

Once you have woken up properly, the hangover will leave you unusually sensitive to smells. Toasted cheese for breakfast is out, but refrain from criticizing anyone else about smells they may create. Remember that, normally, you can only smell about 5 per cent as well as a dog. Today, even the dog doesn't think you smell that good.

Staring

One of the weirdest things associated with a hangover is the way that certain normal, mundane, everyday objects seem to merit close and prolonged observation. They become truly fascinating. The shape and form of a cup, a stapler, your thumb, a shoelace or a pencil sharpener can suddenly become the most enthralling, significant and meaningful thing you have ever seen – so you soak up every intricate detail, endlessly staring at them. Don't do it. You look like a moron.

Sunglasses

Keep a pair by your bedside. Sleep with them on if you can. You never know when some fool might open the curtains or switch on a light.

Strange But True . . .

Next time you pop a ready-meal in the microwave, spare a thought for the Canadian nightwatchman from Thompson in Manitoba who didn't quite understand the nature of microwaves.

Microwaves are absorbed by the moisture inside whatever it is that you are trying to heat. The nightwatchman was working a twelve-hour shift on Christmas Eve and decided to keep warm by sitting in front of a microwave-emitting telecommunications-relay dish. He appeared to have warmed himself this way before and seemed to believe that the dish gave off heat rather than the highly dangerous microwaves. He had a folding chair and a twelve-pack of beer to see him through his stint. During the evening there was a boost in power to ten times normal levels to cope with the increased telecoms traffic expected at Christmas. Unfortunately, no one told the nightwatchman.

He should not, of course, have been sitting in front of the dish anyway, but when the next shift arrived to relieve him in the morning he was still there – roasted to a crisp.

A woman drove me to drink
and I didn't even
have the decency
to thank her.

W. C. FIELDS

The Best Medicine

While you're praying for your hangover to end or praying that the hair-of-the-dog pint you are drinking will cure you, now would be a good time to remember that most solemn of all prayers – The Beer Prayer.

THE BEER PRAYER

Our Lager,
Which ends in hangovers,
Swallowed be Thy game,
Thy swill be drunk,
On draft as it is in bottles.
Give us this day the frothing head,
And forgive us our drunken passes,
As we forgive those who make drunken passes at us,
And lead us not into police stations,
But deliver us from kebab shops,
For Thine is the bitter,
The lager and the Guinness,
Fine ales are forever,
Barmen.

Sure Cure

MORNING GLORY

Yes, it may be a euphemism for something that you'd probably rather not fill your mouth with shortly after waking up, but it's also the name of a hangover cure. Like so many other Sure Cures, the Morning Glory has enough alcohol in it to stun a small elephant, so don't risk trying it out if you're about to get in the car and drive somewhere, even if you're only a passenger.

> 2 measures whisky
> 1 measure absinthe
> 1 egg
> 2 teaspoons cocktail syrup
> Squeeze of lime juice
> 1 slice of lemon

Mix it all in a large glass, then drop in the lemon and drink it as quickly as you dare. Remember to keep your doctor's phone number handy and make sure your will is up to date, just in case.

Teeth

False teeth are very easy to lose when drunk and almost impossible to find when you are hungover. For a start, mumbling 'Hash amygubby sheenma teesh?' while hungover is guaranteed to bewilder anyone in the vicinity sober enough to help. Avoid the problem by tying your teeth on a string round your neck. Those who have all their own teeth should be very careful to avoid cracking their lips when they peel them off their teeth in the morning.

Throat

This feels like you have a very frightened bear cub lodged just behind your tonsils. Why very frightened? Well, it might explain the taste of shit in your mouth.

Thyme Tea

Crush five or six fresh thyme leaves in a cup, add boiling water, cover the cup with a saucer and leave it to infuse for about five minutes. Take out the leaves before you take a sip. Thyme tea works to soothe some people's hangovers and anything's worth a try.

Time

Where the hell did it go? One minute it was time for the next round, the next minute it was time to wake up and go to work. If only Dr Who could open a pub inside his TARDIS.

Toes

The mysterious black and blue spots on your toes are not some form of plague. They were caused by the girl you met in the bar. She stomped her high heels on your feet when you tossed a coin in front of her and asked her what were the chances of getting head.

Toilet

Your new best friend.

Tongue

Usually found in the morning stuck to the roof of your mouth. Once prized free, it will feel twice its normal thickness (see *Ang-naff-nang*).

Trough

As you surf through the rolling waves of your hangover, you will experience highs known as 'peaks' (see *Peaks*). A peak can only exist, sadly, with a trough either side of it. So, whatever you way you look at it, whether you are optimistically climbing towards a peak, or despairingly slipping down into a trough, best keep the bucket handy.

HANGOVERS IN HISTORY

Dallas, America, 1963

There you are. I wondered where you'd got to.

I needed some fresh air by the window.

Me, too. Mind if I join you? I've got a head full of jackhammers.

Sure, pull up a box of books. They're easier to balance on than bar stools.

Ah . . . you saw me take a tumble last night, then?

Yup. I was the one who tried to untangle you from the legs of the stool. Never had to break up a brawl between a man and an item of furniture before.

Don't remind me. Your birthday party turned into a heck of a night.

Yeah. It was the tequila that did for me.

You won the slammer race hands down.

Face down was how I saw it.

You hit that table top pretty hard. We thought your nose would never stop bleeding. Good job the waitress used to be a nurse.

I don't think my date was too impressed.

I guess not. Not many girls find a man attractive when he has a wad of cotton hanging out of each nostril.

Don't suppose she'll want to see me again.

She doesn't want to see me again, either.

You hit on my date?

Only after you hit on the table. She said if I couldn't cope between a bar stool's legs I wasn't getting anywhere near hers.

Did you see him this morning . . . Harvey?

I've been seeing giant pink elephants, not giant white rabbits.

Huh?

You know – Harvey – the white rabbit from that James Stewart movie.

No, I meant the weird guy that works upstairs . . . he's got two first names . . .

Lee Harvey Oswald? Yeah, he went upstairs earlier.

Hey, look out in the square! Here comes President Kennedy's motorcade . . .

Blame It All On The Booze

OUZO

Ouzo . . . you remember . . . it's that weird stuff you had on holiday in Greece that had magical properties. It was clear as a bell until you put a drop of water or an ice cube in it, then it turned white as a ghost and, no matter how deep your suntan was, when you drank the stuff, so did you. It then transported you into another dimension – a parallel universe where your apartment or hotel room was impossible to find and your t-shirt became so heavy that your legs started to buckle. You can always tell someone who's been drinking ouzo; you just can't tell them anything they'll understand. They also smell like they've eaten the contents of a florist's shop window.

The distinctive aroma comes mainly from the anise used to flavour the drink. Ouzo is traditionally drunk by the Greeks along with *mezedes*, which are appetizer snacks such as squid, sardines or fried zucchini. The anise is meant to help the digestive system to cope. Anise is not the only flavouring used in ouzo, though. The raw spirit is distilled from the juice of grapes or raisins and other additives can include coriander, cloves, liquorice, fennel and cinnamon. It's a complex drink with a complex history, having first been produced, or so they claim, by Lesbians.

No, you didn't read that last bit wrong. The Greek island of Lesbos was home to the poet Sappho, who wrote about her great admiration for other women but the people of Lesbos – the Lesbians (stop that sniggering) – also claim to have been the first to produce what is now known as ouzo. The island is still an important centre for the manufacture of ouzo, but the drink's history goes so far back in time that it becomes as murky as the stuff itself.

Ouzo is a relatively modern term for what was once called *tsipouro* and is certainly related to raki. Some say that raki is Turkish and ouzo is Greek but, since the Turks and the Greeks tend to disagree about most things, they inevitably argue that one (their own) is infinitely better than the other. In a blind tasting, the only conclusion you are likely to come to is that you are blind drunk. Both ouzo and raki are also similar to arrak, another drink produced in the eastern Mediterranean and North Africa. The anise flavour also makes for an easy comparison with absinthe and pastis. Absinthe was banned in many countries when it was realized that a certain chemical from the wormwood plant that was used in its manufacture made you go doolally. To avoid all their customers going mad, the French absinthe producers switched to making the less dangerous pastis. The one thing that can be totally guaranteed about all these drinks is that one too many will give you a real corker of a hangover and leave your breath smelling so strongly of liquorice and aniseed that everyone will think you've been snogging Bertie Bassett.

Ugly

This is how you will look. No one looks pretty with a hangover.

Unwanted Phone Calls

These will start to arrive almost as soon as you are awake, mainly in response to the calls you made to let your feelings be known to your ex-girlfriend, your landlord, your MP and your boss when you got home around 2.00 a.m.

Upset

This can apply to your stomach, the pub table you knocked over, the friends who were then drenched in lager, or all three. It does not apply to the sobbing, emotional wreck you turned into on the way home. Grown-ups should not become upset and start to cry just because they can't finish the newspaper sudoku, saw a three-legged dog or buttoned their coat up the wrong way. That's just being drunk.

Veisalgia

This is the proper term for a hangover. It comes from a weird mix of Norwegian and Greek words; *kveis* – meaning 'uneasiness after debauchery' and *algia* – meaning pain.

Vitamin C

You need this. It stimulates the liver to break down alcohol and is vital for your brain to function properly. You get Vitamin C from all sorts of citrus fruit, notably oranges. The camu camu fruit contains up to sixty times more Vitamin C than an orange but, as it is has to be harvested wild in the Amazonian rain forests, it's probably easier to get an orange in Sainsbury's. A note of caution – overloading your system with Vitamin C can give you the scoots (see *Diarrhoea*).

Voice

If all you can manage is a growly, squeaky sound, blame it on the bear cub (see *Throat*).

Vomit

Unless you lost the contents of your stomach the previous evening while still drunk, vomiting can be expected when the hangover really kicks in. Lack of control can make this pretty spectacular – we're talking *The Exorcist* scenes here – so stand well back and fetch a bucket. No matter how much you might feel tempted when overcome with a rising tide of nausea in an inappropriate setting (the boss's office, for example) never feel tempted to clamp your hand over your mouth. This will almost certainly result in a 'five-finger spread' (see *Five-Finger Spread*) and a bill for the redecoration of whatever room you happen to be in.

The Best Medicine

A man is waiting nervously in a hospital side room as his wife gives birth to their first child, and leaps to his feet as a doctor appears. The doctor, however, has bad news. The man's wife has given birth to a boy, but the child has no torso, arms or legs – he is just a head.

The man and his wife care for the boy and raise him as well as they can. On his eighteenth birthday, the man takes his son to the local pub for his first drink. Everyone in the pub toasts the young head on his birthday and his father raises a glass of whisky to his son's lips. No sooner has he taken a sip than, miraculously, he immediately grows a complete torso! There is wild cheering in the pub and the man puts the whisky glass to his son's lips again. Within seconds he has grown two complete arms! With his two new hands the boy quickly grabs the glass and gulps the rest of the whisky. He instantly grows two perfect legs. The pub is in an uproar, with everyone whooping and cheering. Like a young foal, the boy is a little unsteady on his legs and a little drunk from the whisky. He staggers this way and that before stumbling out of the front door into the road where he is hit by a passing bus and killed.

The barman sighs, picks up the empty glass and says, 'That boy should have quit while he was a head.'

Sure Cure

HAIR OF THE DOG II

Although it has come to mean having a drink of whatever it was that gave you the hangover in the first place (see page 35), the Hair of the Dog is also an actual hangover recipe, although like all such recipes, many people have their own variations that include their own special ingredients. You will only find out the best way to prepare a Hair of the Dog through assiduous research and experimentation. The morning of your hangover probably isn't the best time for that, though, so here is one version that you can try out straight away.

> 2 measures of whisky
> 2 measures of double cream
> 1 tablespoon of honey

Mix it all together well and add some ice if you like. When you're struck down with a cold, this one is also good for soothing sore throats.

Wanker

You danced like one of these last night.

Whispering

To cut down on the noise inside your head, you may feel the need to talk in whispers. It will do no good. No one will be able to hear a word you are saying, even though you think you sound just as loud as you were in the pub last night. They will then shout at you in an effort to compensate and that's the last thing you want.

'Why?'

Almost everything you say this morning will begin with this word. Why didn't I go home when I said I would? Why did I stay for just one more drink? Why did I demonstrate Russian dancing on top of the patrol car? Why did I call the driver 'PC Poncypants'? Why is that damned bird tweeting so bloody loudly?

Don't worry too much about the 'Why' syndrome. You will shake off the habit of starting everything with 'Why' by the afternoon and move on to using other familiar phrases (see 'Oh, Noooo . . .').

Wipes

When you've spent so long on the toilet that your bum is moulded into an oval shape you will doubtless also be suffering some degree of tenderness caused by the throughput. It's never a particularly proud boast to say that you can shit through the eye of a needle. Rather than scrub away with normal toilet paper, however, always keep a pack of wipes handy; the kind they use for toilet-training toddlers. These are far kinder to your poor old bum.

Work

No work at all should be attempted while you are hungover. You will only have to do it all again when you are properly sober. If you must go into work, do not let anyone know you have a hangover. You must look as normal as possible, then feign back pain, a knee injury or contact lens trouble to avoid any kind of work. Let the hangover take over in order to give a convincing enough performance to extract maximum sympathy and be sent home. Sadly, this will not work on the day after the office party when everyone will be walking around hunched like Quasimodo, limping like Long John Silver and feeling their way around like Stevie Wonder.

Worms

You can see these grubby things wriggling, shivering and crawling across the table towards your slice of toast. No matter how disgusting they look, don't be tempted to hack at them with the butter knife. They are actually your fingers.

*It takes only one drink to get me drunk.
The trouble is, I can't remember if it's the thirteenth or the fourteenth.*

GEORGE BURNS

Strange But True . . .

Italian Orfeo Agostinetto was a celebrated amateur Italian winemaker from Treviso who would produce up to 500 gallons at a time. He did not die, as might have been expected, from cirrhosis of the liver, although he probably drank a fair bit in passing. Having sampled a few glasses of his latest vintage, Orfeo slipped and fell into a vat containing his new 500-gallon batch. Sadly, with no one around to help him, he drowned.

There is no truth in the rumour that he got out several times to go for a pee.

HANGOVERS IN HISTORY

London, England, 1975

Good morning.

What's good about it?

It's just an expression.

So's 'sod off.'

Now, now, calm down and have some coffee.

Sorry, coffee would be great. I feel like the backside of a punk rocker's pants.

What was that dance you were doing last night?

The pogo.

Very energetic. I've never seen anyone puke quite that far.

Don't remind me. The boss wasn't too happy.

Well, nobody's going to be happy with their shirt and tie covered in lager and blackcurrant vomit.

Why on earth did you let me drink that crap?

You said purple lips made you look like a vampire – and then you bit that PR bloke.

Still, the boss looked pretty cool when he changed into that bin liner.

You took his shirt home to wash it, then?

Yeah, stuffed it in the machine when I got in.

And where did you leave the rest of the votes?

In that bag in the corner.

Yeeeuch!! What a stench!

What is it?

The boss's shirt's in the bag! That means the final votes are . . .

. . . in my washing machine!

Christ! Now we have to take the voting as it stands and that makes *her* the new Conservative Party leader!

Oh, bugger . . . but when the General Election comes around people won't want Margaret Thatcher as Prime Minister . . . will they?

Xerox

If there is a crumpled Xerox photocopy lying near your bed when you wake up, carefully unfold it. Now check in the mirror to see if it's your arse that appears on the photocopy. Now try to figure out who the arse alongside yours belongs to.

Xmas Party

There is no way that you can skive off work the morning after an office Xmas party. Even if you try to phone in, the only people there to take your call will be the Jehova's Witness from Accounts who doesn't drink or someone who was too drunk to find his way out before the doors were locked and wants you to come in and let him go home. It is at this time of year that you come to appreciate the true value of the hair of the dog. It will dull the overwhelming feelings of shame and embarrassment that hit you like a kick from a donkey every so often throughout the day.

X-rated

Often closely related to *Xmas Party* (see above), these are the photographs posted on notice boards, circulated by mobile phone, sent by email and generally broadcast worldwide via NASA satellites to everyone that you would really rather didn't see them. If you're very unlucky, your best man will be using a set as part of his speech on your wedding day. To avoid such embarrassment, always keep your kit on and remember that your tongue was designed exclusively for use in your mouth, not in someone else's . . . or in any other part of their anatomy.

Yawn

Fatigue brought on by lack of sleep will bring on quite a few yawns during the course of the day. A normal yawn is harmless enough, although you should reassure anyone to whom you are talking that they are actually terrifically interesting, but a 'Technicolour Yawn' is another matter (see *Barf*).

Y-fronts

These may well have appeared at *Xmas Party* and *X-rated*. Functional rather than attractive, Y-fronts are one of the garments in your wardrobe that you really shouldn't be seen wearing in public. Especially not on your head.

Yowl

The wolf yowls at the moon. You have the yowl of a wolf. You have the posture of a wolf. But nobody ever saw a wolf with its head down the toilet.

Yuck

Sometimes you find this in your Y-fronts.

Blame It All On The Booze

SANGRIA

It's as Spanish as the sombrero, the straw donkey and the pink lobster suntan, holidaymakers having enjoyed it since Spain first opened up to mass tourism in the 1960s. It can also be a boozer's worst nightmare, bringing on a hangover in the early evening before you would normally even have started getting plastered. The trouble is that sangria goes so well with a seat in the sun, a seat under a shady tree, a seat under a beach umbrella, a seat by the pool or a seat anywhere you fancy. Drinking it standing up is never advisable because you've got too far to fall . . . and that's the second problem. Sangria is beautifully refreshing on a warm afternoon. Sometimes you can get so beautifully refreshed you can barely stand. There's no telling what's gone into your sangria, you see. It could be little more than a wine-tainted fruit cocktail, or it might have a kick stronger than a bad-tempered burro. It all depends on what has gone into making it. One thing's for sure: if you've had a few glasses in the afternoon followed by a nap on a sun lounger, you can easily wake up with a premature hangover that will blight your whole evening.

Sangria is a kind of wine punch, the recipe for which can vary wildly from one beach bar or nightclub to another. The basic recipe includes a bottle of red wine; a spoonful of honey or cocktail syrup; an orange, peeled and chopped; a lemon, peeled and chopped; a couple of measures of brandy; a couple of measures of Cointreau; a glass of club soda or lemonade and a stack of ice cubes. You let everything bar the lemonade or soda and the ice mingle together in a large jug for a while so that the flavours blend. This is best done in a fridge to keep it all cool. Then you add the fizzy drink and the ice.

The potency of the sangria obviously depends on the strength of the wine and the amount of spirits that are added but it's so easy to drink that you can easily be fooled into thinking that it's a perfectly harmless concoction, so be on your guard.

Sangria is also made with white wine, which is called *sangria blanca* and in some parts of Spain it is made with peaches and called *zurra*. Some recipes use both red and white wine and in some bars there is sangria on tap, although this is more likely actually to be *tinto de verano*, a kind of chilled red wine spritzer served with ice and lemon.

In Spain you are most likely to be served sangria in a large jug, but at parties it can be served in a large bowl with a ladle, just like punch. Either way, the fruit content can include the basic orange and lemon mix, or it can have bananas, apple, strawberries, nectarines and all manner of other fruit floating around. Normally people drink the mixture without pouring the fruit or the ice in their glass, but you might as well let the fruit come tumbling out of the jug, too. If you're going to have an early evening sangria hangover, you'll need all of the vitamins you can get!

The Best Medicine

A bloke waiting to meet his friend in a pub finds himself at the bar next to a pretty girl and can't quite believe his luck. Even when he tries out a few of his lame, ice-breaker quips she responds well and he starts to think he might be in with a chance.

'So what's your name?' he asks her.

'Carmen,' she replies.

'That's an unusual name,' he comments. 'Are you named after your mother?'

'No,' she says, 'I decided on this name myself.'

'Really?' he says. 'Why Carmen?'

'Because I like cars and I like men,' she smiles, pouting at him. 'What's your name?'

'Lagershag.'

Sure Cure

THE FRANKENSTEIN

So called because it can reputedly re-animate apparently lifeless bodies, The Frankenstein will either be your salvation or it will turn you into a creature that strongly resembles Dr F's bolt-necked creation. There are as many corpse-reviver recipes around as there are miserably hungover wretches to try them out. Like the other alcohol-based Sure Cures, this may slide you swiftly back into the cosy womb of inebriation where you feel no pain, rather than actually curing your hangover. What the hell . . . if you're reading this you obviously like the odd drink or two anyway.

> 1 measure calvados
> 1 measure cognac
> 1 measure sweet vermouth
> 1 slice of lemon

Pour it all into a glass over ice cubes, stir and squeeze a wedge of lemon into it before adding the wedge itself. Remove all breakable objects from your immediate vicinity before drinking.

A TO Z OF HANGOVERS Z

Zzzzzzzzzz

Zeds are what you really need. The best possible hangover cure is to drink as much water as you can get down your neck, have a light snack and sleep it off. Your body will then sort itself out while you dream about saying all those smart and witty things you were too drunk and slow to say the night before. A sleeping dream is like an interactive action replay where you can change what happens, although sometimes it can get completely out of control. There were no Cybermen in the pub and you did not defeat them by pouring cider in their ears.

Zip

Catching your foreskin in it when you're doing up your flies means a trip to the hospital and possible circumcision. If you don't have a foreskin, it's even worse. Be careful out there.

Zombie

In the film *Shaun of the Dead*, the zombies were outside the pub smashing their way in. Strangely, last night it was the other way round . . .

Zoned-Out

Another effect associated with intense concentration on an everyday object that really doesn't merit such attention (see *Staring*). When you are zoned-out, however, the object needn't be sitting right in front of you. Being zoned-out can leave you staring at a mundane artefact that is actually anything up to several thousand miles away.

Zonked

When you are zonked you are in a state of perilous fatigue. One moment you are listening to a perfectly reasonable conversation and the next your chin is on your chest and there's a snail trail of dribble heading for your belly button. The dangerous part is when the zonking catches you leaning ever so slightly backwards when all the fluid in your skull seems to rush to the rear and your head snaps back with neck-breaking violence. A neck brace like those worn by car-crash whiplash victims is the answer. It elicits genuine sympathy from others while allowing you to nod off in complete safety.

Zoroastrianism

You could explain this ancient Persian religion in great detail in the pub last night. Now you can't even say it.

Zulu

Great film. Get it on DVD and watch it with tea and toast as a hangover cure. Don't worry if you nap for a while. Just rewind. Michael Caine really doesn't mind.

I formed a new group called
Alcoholics Unanimous.
If you don't feel like a drink,
you ring another member
and he comes over
to persuade you.

RICHARD HARRIS